This Is Reading

FRANK G. JENNINGS

Bureau of
Publications

*Teachers College
Columbia University*

New York • 1965

For

Lou LaBrant

great teacher, gallant lady,
excellent scholar—maker of
good teachers.

Beyond the usual declarations of conjugal support, it must be recorded that my wife, Gloria, provided whatever editorial stability there is to be found in these pages.

FGJ

Foreword

Reading is a many-faceted subject. A book on the topic may, like many, be a description of the physiological steps one takes in performing the process called reading. More commonly, it is a manual, describing the methods a teacher may use in teaching schoolage children to acquire the mechanical aspects of reading. Some, far fewer, are focused on the psychology of reading, such psychology usually emphasing the conscious and logical approaches to learning. Still others are directed toward some particular part of reading in its socio-historical setting, as for example, freedom to read, or adult reading habits, or variation in trends in the production of materials. All books of such nature are relevant to the omnibus topic—reading.

A book which would include reading in its historical, sociological, and educational setting would indeed be a major undertaking, demanding both scope and depth of knowledge from its author. Frank Jennings has written such an inclusive book, and he appropriately calls it *This Is Reading*.

Concern for the quality and function of reading in child and adult life, often regarded as the sole property of the educator, is properly treated as a family-centered and community-wide, as well as a school, matter. Therefore *This Is Reading* is a book for parents, lay readers and educators. The historical sweep from early use of symbols to the present time, the key role which symbols in general and certain books in particular have played and the deep psychological ramifications in how one selects what he reads today, this broad scope is not only lucidly presented, but also kept in focus so that the effect of reading on the individual is in the foreground.

Frank Jennings writes with verve, pungent phrases and sharp-edged examples. He has the breadth and profoundness of scholarship to draw upon, so his book is punctuated with many references to his own background of reading. Because of his style, clear understanding of any thread of this rich, written tapestry can be followed while reading with ease. Read in its entirety, *This Is Reading* offers a much needed philosophy or outlook on reading essential at this time. From it a parent can acquire a helpful outlook toward his child's reading, a teacher can capture an adequate sense of direction in teaching, a librarian will acquire added zest for expanding library resources, a citizen may re-examine his concern for the work of the schools.

To quote from Frank Jennings' own conclusion: "The more competent readers a society has, the greater will be its capacity for doing good to itself." This audacious book, through myriads of suggestions and examples, stirs a reader to start work promptly in developing such competent readers.

Roma Gans

West Redding, Conn.
November, 1964

Preface

Teaching is the most dangerous profession. It deals with our children, the most precious of our natural resources. It refines them into brave and wonderful adults or it grossly degrades them into dull, over-aged adolescents. Its results color, mold, and determine the shape of our nation and the character of our people.

IF our teachers lack luster, fewer of their charges will be as bright as they might have been. IF our teachers are cowards, they will teach their cowardice.

IF teachers are not responsible citizens, they will produce political idiots. IF teachers become the tools of any pressure group, rather than the prime artisans of a creative society, then we will all shrink into a nation of domesticated, two-legged cattle, capable of nothing but ignorant brutality toward each other and cud-chewing obedience to the loudest shouters and the best feeders.

IF teachers do not earn and keep the status and the respect which their profession requires, their role will be captured by the practical, committed, dedicated members of the industrial and commercial communities, who can train people very well, but who cannot afford the expense of the humane adventure.

Thus, teaching must forever live in creative danger, but teachers must hold onto the protective warnings of these terrifying IF's, lest these warnings become irremovable realities.

It is our great good fortune that in most of the schools in this country many pupils are met by a person for whom the magic of real respect and true love can quickly develop. This is so whether that teacher faces a kindergarten of five-year-olds or a seminar of graduate students. Yet sometimes this magic dies because that teacher is beset by fears and half-understood anxieties that come from the half-empty pocketbook or a half-shattered self-esteem.

The great teacher possesses a personality strong enough to free himself from these pressures. And it is this free teacher who is truly an artist in human relations. (This is something that must not be confused with some teachers college workshop courses bearing the same name.)

Pupil and teacher begin their relationship by studying and learning *each other*. They learn by their common experience to value and to use each other's words and acts and ideas. A group of human beings so learning is the closest to Eden we can ever be. For the interests of young people can encompass the whole world. All kinds of experience press in upon them. The teacher has to know when and how to teach them to begin to be selective about these experiences.

There is great danger here! What happens if our young people are denied the ability to make and to know that they are making significant choices? George Orwell's Big Brother will come and do it for them. To prevent Big Brother from taking over, the teacher has to know and be able to show all the kinds of choices there are. To do this he must have an unquenchable thirst for delight, an insatiable appetite for wonder, and the talent to transmit these qualities to the children.

This is asking more than is ordinarily possible for anyone. But our society must ask this of its teachers. For there is this warning: the teacher who does not love poetry does a rather poor job of arranging a love-affair between words and the child. A teacher for whom all painting beyond the merely pictorial is nonsense cannot follow the child into the rain-forest of color and shapes that is the possible world of that child. A teacher who can think only on one level of understanding at a time cannot keep his bearings amidst the busy questions of thirty thirsty minds. A teacher who does not enjoy reading teaches this lack of enjoyment far more successfully than he can ever teach the rudimentary reading skills a young child requires.

The child learns many things quickly and permanently. Throughout childhood he is learning to be at home in this world, learning to read its signs and portents, learning its firms, unshifting names and the volatile, shifting symbols, learning to listen and to know and to understand, learning to act less on impulse and more with purpose. And of course it is true that he begins to learn all this at home.

Whatever the quality of these home experiences may be, we ask the schools to take up these beginnings and carry them on toward those necessary goals we have set for education. The good teacher must be a person with a profound love of a subject, born of the fullness of familiarity. He must have an excellent operational understanding of basic educational principles, not the mere word-shadows of professional jargon. The teacher must have the ability to awaken and to maintain the interest of students and to direct those interests toward successful experiences. Above all, the teacher must be able to foster wonder.

This is the kind of teacher our society needs. The kind of teaching that teacher is capable of is an acquired skill. Such teachers are born in classrooms. The skill they must have can be learned by anyone with adequate intelligence who is willing to accept the hazards and the dangers of acting upon clearly accepted responsibilities.

Let the cowards and the dullards find safety in the tenure trap! The true teacher joyfully accepts the call of strange tomorrows, finds security and immortality in the healthy, happy, and intelligent citizens he has helped to shape.

FRANK G. JENNINGS

The above appeared as a guest editorial in The Saturday Review, *March 8, 1958.*

Contents

This Is Reading

Part One

1

What Is Reading?

What is reading? Where does it start? How can it be done well? With these questions you can make a fortune, wreck a school system or get elected to the board of education. Most people who try to think about reading at all conjure up these little black wriggles on a page and then mutter something about "meaning." If this is all it is, very few of us would ever learn anything. For reading is older than printing or writing or even language itself. Reading begins with wonder at the world about us. It starts with the recognition of repeated events like thunder, lightning and rain. It starts with the seasons and the growth of things. It starts with an ache that vanished with food or water. It occurs when time is discovered. Reading begins with the management of signs of things. It begins when the mother, holding the child's hand says that a day is "beautiful" or "cold" or that the wind is "soft." Reading is "signs and portents," the flight of birds, the changing moon, the "changeless" sun and the "fixed" stars that move through the night. Reading is the practical management of the world about us. It was this for the man at the cave's mouth. It is this for us at the desk, the bench or control panel.

The special kind of reading that you are doing now is the culmination of all the other kinds of reading. You are dealing with the signs of the things represented. You are dealing with ideas and concepts that have no material matter or substance and yet are "real." But you can not do this kind of reading if you have not become skilled in all the other kinds. Unless you know down from up, hot from cold, now from then, you could never learn to understand things that merely represent other things. You would have no language, as you now understand it, and you could not live in the open society of human beings. It is quite conceivable that a true non-reader can only survive in a mental hospital.

For most of the world's people the act of reading what is written down is still surrounded with an aura of mystery and the black arts. Throughout most of our history reading has been the prerogative of elite classes. Its earliest practitioners were priests and their special agents. The terrible power of the "remembering line" of writing held kings in bondage and made wisdom a commodity for sale at the temple. The owner of the book was the possessor of strong magic and so was respected, or feared, which amounted to the same thing. But the man who could wrest from a book its core of meaning and make it completely his own, was still stronger. The Egyptian god Horus, as a child, was able to possess the "wisdom" of a scroll merely by touching it. Everyone who hopes or wishes for some magical way of committing the printed word to understanding memory, without a struggle, is repeating the essence of this myth.

Until the beginning of the twentieth century, reading was thought of as a simple unitary act. Books were to be "mulled over," "studied" and struggled with. The teaching of reading was begun as a sort of matching game in which the child was trained to fit appropriate symbols together, beginning with the letters and building up to words and sentences. The child's formal introduction to the joys of reading began with the line, "A is for Adam. In Adam's fall, sinned we all." Here was a somber and sobering thought for the tyke. It was guaranteed to get rid of any notion that there ought or might be pleasure in reading.

The reading habits of any age are the direct products of the pressures of society and the world in which we live. You can easily see this in the ways in which we have used reading in this country. During colonial days and immediately thereafter in education, religion dominated the drama of life. The literature of the Bible and other kinds of religious writing provided almost all of the reading material available for most of the people. Some writers of the history of reading say that this kind of reading fulfilled a "felt need" (a favorite and not inaccurate phrase of many educators). They say that because of the hostile environment of the day-to-day struggle for some kind of security, man became sensitive to his spiritual resources. This is probably a superficial reading of our social history, but it is true that when all of the people, except for the usual cranks and subversives keep their thoughts on God and their eyes on the acts of their neighbors, most people wouldn't be caught with anything other than an approved text. When the approvers happened to be New England divines who were quick with torch, rope and dunking stool, the intelligent and the wise would repair to the good book. And since pleasure whelped sin, they wisely suffered as they read.

This, of course was not true of all of the people, or even of some of the people all of the time. You have to read secular instructions if you are to survive in a world of waves and wilderness. You have to get the clear meaning out of what is written down if you are anxious to avoid financial or physical disaster. Road signs say their piece only once. The governor's edict in declarative prose had to be understood and acted upon. People in the colonies were busy trying to break even with life, so they had little time for reading that was not utilitarian.

The Industrial Revolution turned a lot of things upside-down, including our reading habits, and our notion of the proper place and function of religion. The New England theocracy was bound to shatter on the rock-bound coast of opportunity in the new world. If religion were to continue to suppress rather than to support the interests and capacities of man it would be ditched for a kinder contact with God, so religion, always willing, however reluctantly, to meet the "felt needs" of the people, turned a little toward the light and said that it was good. More and more, there was evidence that faith in the value of secular knowledge paid handsome dividends and more and more writers and speakers of influence announced that the printed word was in fact a safeguard against the corrosive

influences of ignorance. Under the pressure of this kind of publicity
many people read many books that their grandfathers would have
burned, along with the reader, writer and publisher. The announcement of moral standards was no longer the central service sought
from the book. Men wanted to know things and facts and if the
book could instruct them, they would read.

Long before the middle of the nineteenth century, publishing in
the United States had become a flourishing industry. Without the
let or hindrance of copyright and with the aid of translators of
widely varying talent, a flood of books carrying the world's knowledge was washed across the country. The hindsight of history always
makes us out to be splendid solvers of jigsaw puzzles. With an
expanding agrarian economy as a background and the bright light
of an apparently limitless frontier to illumine the board, the pieces
fell into their appointed places. In the last half of the nineteenth
century, daily newspapers flourished. Public and private libraries
were set up in the smallest cities. Jefferson's notion of appropriate
educational opportunities was considerably expanded and public instruction in literacy was accepted as a social responsibility. Science
was getting its hands dirty in mine and mill, filling the purses of
the enterprising. The kind of power that was respected and sought
was the kind that moved and made things and the knowledge of
this power was eminently democratic. It required no school tie, no
proper family connection, only an eagerness to know, a willingness
to seek out the little truths that turned wheels and lighted the dark
houses. With this explosive expansion of the desire for and the use
of knowledge there came too, a recognition of the obligation of
anyone who would be anybody, to read widely and skillfully. So,
although the teaching of the alphabet might still be a key to the
library's treasure, it was a shining, inviting instrument, promised
joys to children, pride for the parents and the world's riches for the
whole community.

But change and development have always been most characteristic
of the American community. And there have been enormous
changes in our world during the last half-century. As Dr. La Brant

said, "It would be absurd to think that the methods and purposes in the teaching and the learning of reading have not also changed with our world." [1] Until this century, reading, talking and actual demonstration were the only ways in which information could be transmitted. Now we get our information and our entertainment from many sources. The world of words in which we are immersed is so radically different from that of our grandfathers' and even our fathers' that some of them have been overwhelmed and have been forced to retreat from it. In many ways our children are living on a planet that differs from the one we knew.

It all began innocently enough, in the "good old American way" of competition. The news had to be gotten to the public more quickly, the public had to be wooed with flashy, easy-to-read pages, excited and stimulated by any means to read and later to look at one paper, one magazine above all others. The end product is the picture magazine that puts almost no strain upon the literacy of its purchaser and the tabloid newspaper that reduces current events to slogans, nicknames and exclamations.

Mergenthaler made it easy with his linotype machine, but the tramp printer had already started things with his lightning fingers, and a hundred gadgeteers and inventors brought mass production to printing long before anyone else suspected it could be applied to factory work.

A word-avalanche was started in the late days of the nineteenth century that built up the pressures that created the needs for more and more information, faster and faster. The telegraph and the telephone wiped out distance between towns, and made and shrank time into the tight little ball of the present. The moving picture, spawned out of electricity, silver nitrates and celluloid, followed an ancient Chinese injunction about words and pictures, and compressed an experience of a lifetime into a matter of minutes. There was a new kind of reading that had to be learned here, but it was

[1] Lou La Brant, "Personal Factors in Reading," in William S. Gray, Editor, *Reading in an Age of Mass Communication*, New York: Appleton Century Crofts, 1949, p. 56.

learned quickly since the skills required were not far removed from those of watching the old shadow plays or the more recent jack-o-lantern.

There was a pause of brooding power as the new century dawned. Scientists and tinkerers were toying with strange new invisible waves, and the way the earth's atmosphere reacted to them. Edison's electric lamp made electrons behave oddly and the galvanic secret of the compass needle became common knowledge. Count Rutherford made electric sparks jump little gaps, as had Franklin long before him, but then the Italian, Tesla, made a veritable Jovian bolt, and his compatriot, Marconi, used it to hurl words across the Atlantic.

Man, it seems is always trying to make his words go farther, loom larger and stay longer. This last skill he learned early and so invented history. For the others, he had used everything from pigeons and kites, to cupped hands, billboards, megaphones and pulpits. But it wasn't until 1920, when radio station KDKA went on the air with the results of the presidential elections that the world of words began to envelop the earth.

For a generation the phonograph had sung songs to the nation but it was a readily domesticated instrument. It didn't stop the family from living its life as usual. Now with the dancing electrons pounding into private earphones, the family, as individuals, was tied to and transfixed by a little black box. They sat through the night and listened for sense through squawks and squeals and whistles. They stopped talking. They stopped reading. A newborn radio trade magazine noted in the early 1920's, "The rate of increase of the number of people who spend at least a part of their evening in listening is almost incomprehensible . . . . It seems quite likely that before the movement has reached its height . . . there will be at least five million receiving sets in this country." This sounds like warnings about post-war television. The youngsters were shooed off to bed and the parents braved the chill quiet of the night to be able to brag the next morning of having "pulled in" a station three hundred miles away.

During this whole period public education was becoming more public. Although sanctioned by law as available to all, less than 700,000 boys and girls were enrolled in high schools in 1900. But when KDKA went on the air, that number had climbed to almost two and one half million, and by 1930 it had reached six and one half million. Of course it is true that our total population has also doubled in this period, but the point for all pundits to consider is that up to 1900 the high school was a highly selective institution in which only those possessing high verbal skills could hope to survive. It was in fact a preparatory school for our intellectual elite. Today, although we still tend to judge intelligence in terms of verbal proficiency, we are committed to the proposition that all America's youth have opportunities to develop and learn a wide variety of skills that will enable them to be full-functioning citizens in our communities.

Now this is a grand commitment, fully worthy of such a nation as ours. It is the substance from which we draw much moral strength as well as our seemingly limitless production and creative powers; but the specter of the New England schoolman haunts us. When we look in upon ourselves and consider what we are, we see an image that is not cast by a student's lamp but by an acetylene torch. We are as brawling and as sprawling as Whitman and Frost and Sandburg have seen us. We are at once rough and subtle, but the brawn bulks larger and we are self-conscious, ashamed.

What is the first thing that we do to a newborn child? We talk to it. We wrap it round with a welter of sound before its brain can sort out any of the reports of its senses. We interpret any wriggle or squawk as a sign that we are understood. This gives us immense satisfaction, and at the beginning it costs the child nothing since it hasn't yet learned to be confused. Not until it becomes aware of confusion and seeks to get rid of it, does it begin to function in ways we like to call human, but from the very beginning the rest of us are in frantic haste that it should be aware of us and the world. We want this awareness so that we may act as human beings toward the child and the difficulties that we and it are confronted with in reaching such a point can only be resolved when some level of understanding is reached.

Put very simply, this means we are trying to talk to the infant. We have trouble from the very beginning—first because he doesn't know and later because he won't pay attention. Notice too that "it" has become a male child on whom it is easier to heap the sins of omission and commission than on a girl. We have trouble getting through to him and later on that trouble increases in direct proportion as we try to help him understand. And then the school steps in and the critics howl: they say that the trouble multiplies because teachers are not anywhere nearly as professional at teaching as parents are at "parenting." Schools have been following a descending scale of performance at least since Socrates. Most parents know from experience that the schools are not as good as they used to be. "Why, when I was in high school, everybody was a good reader!" "We never wasted time on trips and games the way they do today." "Imagine, promoting a child because it is old enough for the next grade!" It is probably because of the nature of education in a democratic society that everyone feels called upon to say something about it. There have been more committees and commissions on the problems of education in the last twenty years than on most of the other institutions in our society. Everyone wants to get into the act.

Our language heritage, misread in the nineteenth century parlors appears still to hold us to the adventures of the written word, to the battle of books. Despite all we know and it is a very great deal, we as a people can be thrown into a panic by a garrulous and argumentative scholar, new to our language and ignorant of our usage, who looks through the wrong end of his research telescope and discovers a little boy who doesn't "read" his mother tongue with the polished skill that he, an adult foreigner has acquired.

As a nation of educators, and we are that as surely as the antique Greeks ever were, we know a vast amount about what learning is and what it entails. We make and have made mistakes, but that's the asking price of adventure and experiment. When we realized that the three R's were necessary but not sufficient for the full de-

velopment of our children, we went overboard in our practice sometimes, although our more competent philosophers and guides were
more cautious than us in their theories. We have liberated our
children even as the very shape of the family was being changed
by packaged foods and the automobile. We have produced generations which, for all their mistakes, have done things that no legend
dared imagine. And we have done this by teaching our children to
read.

But reading, remember, is not restricted to the printed page. Actually it never was. In one sense reading *is* the art of transmitting the
ideas, facts and feelings from the mind and soul of an author to the
mind and soul of a reader, with accuracy and understanding, and
much more. But throughout his history man has "read" many
things: the flight of birds, the guts of sheep, sun spots, liver spots
and the life lines on a hand. He has read the lore of the jungle, the
spoor of the beast and the portents in a dish of tea. But whatever
he has read and however he has read, it has always been for "reason."
It was only when man invented symbols for the words in his mouth
and the ideas in his teeming brain that other kinds of reading
became useful, possible or even desirable. Yet even then, as it still in
a large measure is today, this kind of reading was essentially magical.
It was and is converted to practical use when man realized that
words written down could pin down his purposes, hold his plans
still, the better to study and understand them. Word magic is one
of man's most wonderful and most dangerous tools. It builds air
castles, raises an army of dragon men, fixes a star on a name and
sends human blood running through dirty gutters.

Reading begins at the womb when the body first senses the universe, and the message center of the brain scans the scrambled
reports of the senses. Reading gains precision as the sign of an ache
or an emptiness is correctly translated into appropriate and soothing
action. Reading gains in scope when faces and features become organized into personalities. Reading begins to encompass that universe
when the mother, standing with the child at the window, "reads"
the beauty of the day.

Now this is using "reading" in a very odd way; what I'm discussing here might well be called "life-orientation." We can play such useful games with the written and the spoken word. The point is that without this orientation, we cannot have a healthy human being, capable of the mind-taxing disciplines required by the special kind of reading you now are doing.

There are many skills that go to make an efficient reader of printed words. Some are psychological, some are physical, others are social. None can be slighted. The teaching of reading should begin as early as possible, never sooner. It is fully within the range of human capacities to produce an intellectual monster of three or four years who can make the sounds represented by printed words. It is a mark of the toughness of the human personality that some such man-made monsters can survive as relatively whole persons able to live in the society of their fellows. But even as the Biblical sages knew, there is a time for everything and things are best accomplished in their season. So it is with this reading. The schools call it "readiness." The child who has been prepared shows it by a willingness, an eagerness to learn.

But the secret is in the preparation. For too long in this country, probably because of the general excellent of the schools, parents have more and more relinquished their own peculiar responsibilities towards preparing their children for what they want and expect.

The Harvard Committee in their report, *General Education in a Free Society,* observed that:

A child brought up where books are read, interests are in the air, and promptings everywhere solicit his own small explorations will evidently stand a better chance of exhibiting intelligence, as our society judges it, than one who has felt no such promptings.[1]

The learned committee is dealing with the special case but after all this is the one kind of reading we usually have to talk about, so far as the parents are concerned. Because of our traditional interest in the academic aspects of education and because of the relative

[1] *General Education in a Free Society,* Cambridge, Mass.: Harvard University Press, 1946, p. 10.

ease with which achievement in this area can be seemingly gauged by the non-professional, it has been the proverbial touchstone for anxiety and hysteria and in recent years a source of wealth for the unscrupulous, the gadget-minded and the educational confidence-men.

We are a paper and ink civilization. Before and after we are anything else, we are *that*. We scribble notes from the day we learn how to mar wallpaper to the terrible moment when we affix our signatures to the last amended codicil to the final version of our ultimate will and testament. We consume a mountain of print before we die, for amusement, for escape, for enlightenment and for living. And we do all of this usually without ever pausing to wonder at many things. In this nation especially, this wonderment often degenerates into an obsession. If the obsession is diet, we'll eat anything from hay to marbles. If it's "peace of mind" we'll mumble Coué's formula or Peale's positive apostrophe—but today our abiding obsession is with reading. Look at the explosive growth of reading clinics, the do-it-yourself books that offer the same services more cheaply and even less legitimately, the damn-their-eyes books that accuse the teacher, on *misread evidence,* of preventing the child from reading at all. Consider the doleful report of the American Book Publishers Council, ". . . reading is still unattractive to the majority." Yes, something must be done about this . . .

I suspect that it might be a sociological axiom that every such obsession creates a kind of commodity vacuum into which the gadget makers rush with their wonder tools, or tricks, or drugs. Scrabble begets a Scrabble Lazy Susan and even a Scrabble Dictionary. The capable householder becomes a do-it-yourself man with more power tools than his housebuilder ever needed. And so it is with reading. There are kits that are marketed in bookstores. There are correspondence courses too. We have a gadget that pushes the child's nose down the page at the prescribed rate and another that whips his eyes back and forth with the speed of a sidewinder's tail. We have films that make him scan, skip and skim and cameras to picture his eyes' fixations. All we lack is a pill to make him want to read . . . Oh, but we will make him read all right! We have only to organize our know-how, tool up for production and then get the ad men to compose the appropriate incantations.

Reading difficulties are much easier to see than social or psychological problems. A fifth-grade boy who cannot manage a third-grade reader appears to be in much more difficulty than a well-behaved classmate who masters intellectual skills easily, is complaisant and apparently content to be left alone. The very good boy can be in very bad shape. Saying this, however is to throw a sop to some educationists, a goad to some psychological cranks and in general to commit the same pathetic fallacy that the destructive critics of the schools are usually guilty of.

No single facet of human behavior can ever explain the whole personality. It is tempting to seek one, but if one were to exist, the personality in which it was found would be less human because of its existence. The uniqueness of man is the variety of his interests, his goals, his behavior. The wonder of the universe is its multiplicity. Man seeks single answers. This is his passion for neatness. This is how he reaches nearer the angels, how he sees God. But for everyday affairs of life he must blind himself to other possibilities, to see the world in terms of black and white, right and wrong. This too he must do in order to act, or else he must spend his life in paralyzed indecision. The "crazy, mixed-up kid" asks too many questions. The mature adult has made an armed truce with life in order to find the small and partial answers that mean food, shelter and sanity.

"My child can't read," says the troubled parent. "They are not teaching him properly." A visit to the school confirms the fear. Half a dozen groups of children, reading books of varying difficulty may be scattered about the room. Some children may "only" be looking at pictures. The teacher may be working with one group on the recognition and association of words with things and actions. Depending on the age and experience of the group, she may be helping them take words apart and put them together. She may be urging some to read aloud. She may be trying to persuade others not to pronounce the words as they read silently. She may move to another group and talk with them about the story and she may even allow the talk to drift off on tangents of personal remembrances.

The puzzled and worried parent who does not or cannot understand the teacher's explanations of what is going on, will have fears confirmed and may turn for solace and advice to someone who chants the song of the "good old days."

There are basic skills that must be acquired, of course. There are fundamentals to be absorbed, but so it is in every area of human endeavor. A particular kind of knowledge is good for dealing with a particular kind of information. There was once a notion which fortunately continues to have currency, more in the colleges than in the schools, that the learning of Latin or Greek or mathematics somehow "trained" the mind to deal with life problems. The survivors of this "classical" education often achieved considerable success in society. And so that kind of education gained and maintained a reputation for social inefficiency that in fact it never contained.

There has always been a kind of hidden or secret education that goes on whenever people deliberately try to teach skills or knowledge to others. It has become open and purposeful in the last generations. It has always been the actual source of human excellence. It has nothing to do with subject matter, although it uses all knowledge. It is dependent on no specific teaching method, although it experiments with methodology. It has no completely articulated "philosophy of education," although philosophers who are concerned with education tend to agree about general goals and values. This kind of education exists just because some people want to help others to learn to think, to live. They are the wonderful few who have themselves learned how to excite in others the desires to "find out for themselves." They are the ones who can make the dissection of frogs "come alive," who can make the mixed-up mutterings of ancient poets "make sense"; who can make it important that the stars be counted; who can make man's interminable difficulties with himself and others a source of adventure and a cause for hope. They teach people to ask questions, to accept every answer as provisional, to rely for practical affairs only on the kind of information that anyone can get to and check. The students of these teachers learn to think purposefully and solve real problems. They may, incidentally, learn to speak Greek.

In one sense we are all Texans. We go "whole hog" whether it's busting the atom or denying the existence of hard liquor. And we are always nursing a hangover from one or another of our binges. We even invented mass advertising so that we could keep up the noise level on our tricks. We made something called elementary education a free gift of all to each, then we made it compulsory; then we added more education and some of us aren't fazed by the notion of life-long education free for all to the extreme limits of individual needs, urges and desires.

We have a nationwide concern that all be educated. We will not abide a nationwide operation of that institution. We are anxious to give or get help, as the case may be, but no strings attached! We have a naive and abiding faith that education will solve all social personal ills, but then we join groups to keep the schools absolutely free from every influence except ours. We expect our children to be turned into citizens who are as good as or better than we are. Yet when the schools, which we develop, make timid but professional suggestions about how this might be done, we imagine that the foundations of society are tottering. "Keep sex out of the schools." "Keep God in the classroom." "Don't hunt for the skeletons in our historical closets." "Make the children civic-minded but don't make them nosey." "Teach them to be objective about other ways of living." "Teach them to accept the American Way."

Most people are intimidated by professionals. The dentist might be a political moron but we'll accept his judgment on dental affairs until it is contradicted by a physician, or the corner druggist. We assume, usually rightly, a high level of technical competence in our professional people; all but the teachers.

Teachers are not professional, they're—well, they're teachers. In a way, we're in the same business. You had the kids, we handle them. But you were there first, so—so you can talk, and you do, as you should. But whereas a physician can diagnose a non-existent ulcer and you will properly behave as an ulcer-owner, you greet a teacher's suggestion about child care or family relations with suspicion or even contempt.

In a way your attitude is not unwarranted. Many teachers and many of their organizations are status-hungry. They want to be respected. They whimper about their need in staff room, conference room and church socials. They cry poor-mouth in the presence of bank clerks and do the weak-sister act before a trade unionist. They are seedy-looking and faceless, the very spit-and-image of the thing no honest teacher ever was or could be. They can be panicked by an equally under-paid professor of education or a child psychologist on a dry run. So they are fair game for you, but hunting them only hurts your child.

Where human learning is concerned there is no one best way of doing anything, but for the professional person, there are always certain ways that are more appropriate than others. No two children can be made to want to read in the same way. Most children come to school eager to learn everything. But what you have done with and for them in the years before will determine what things they are most anxious to learn. As the Harvard committee pointed out, a child surrounded by an atmosphere rich with the joys of reading, will want to read. One who has come from a home that is barren of books, in which reading by the parents rarely goes beyond the comics and the sport sections of the papers, is hardly going to think very much of the idea of "reading" a story he can see on television. His parents won't be reading this book. Yet our society has decided that he be given reading skills so that he can take full advantage of his "unalienable rights." Where the teacher is faced with one or a few such children in the classroom, her task isn't insurmountable. But where, in addition she has children who for many other reasons, are not either ready or willing to learn to read, then the whole class may be in for difficult times.

Our literary heritage—the wit, wisdom and knowledge of the world's civilizations—is the rightful possession of every child, but some will never claim that inheritance. Yet even they will share in the riches of others. How they will share will depend to a large measure on where they are born, how they grow, who loves them, what they become.

See the conflict here. This is the province of all. The domain of human enterprise. All are called but some do not choose to heed. They are not the less for the choice, nor necessarily the poorer. This world machine of ours is a wonderful servant, far more dependable than the dreamed of genie. Not only has it made books talk. It makes them be. It teaches without tears.

Let us face this fact: There are, there have been and there will be in increasing numbers, boys and girls who will grow up in this country with little in the way of reading skills. They learn how to make out directions. They can read road signs, price tags and the myriad labels that name our world. They will be word-minded only in the simple social sense. Not that they could not have been otherwise, but we fortunately still refuse to make a person become even what would benefit him most. These children will grow, as they have in the past, into full-functioning citizens, fully able to share, and willingly sharing, the burdens of that citizenship. They in turn will rear children, pay taxes, engage in our common defense, contribute to some of our arts. They will neither read nor write books.

In the recent past and today, we have not been serving these people as well as they serve us. They keep wheels going. They make power flow. They make the machines behave. They sing for us. They paint. They even make us laugh. The only thing they cannot do is make the printed and written word behave. What have we given them, we who prefer and know the use of the printed word? Consider television, the film, display advertising, the theatre. These are their major avenues of enlightenment, instruction, entertainment and escape. The words are there, in the air or behind the scenes.

Words are expendable; that is the nature of language. Their meanings wear out and shift. They lose their bite and punch and precision. But words are devalued before their time by the truncated thinking that produces sentences such as, "What type shoes do you want?" "This cigarette is milder." "Let's finalize this contract."

When words are cut off from the things and acts which they are used to refer to, the thinking that they are meant to express becomes confused and crippled. The words are debased!

The attitude that fosters this, however, doesn't start on Madison Avenue, although it ends there. It begins, for example, with an off-hand publicity release from an important university about some research on ways, other than reading, of getting basic information. This release is picked up by a responsible newspaper whose careful headline writer understands the sense of the story to mean "PICTURES HELD TO RIVAL WORDS." The newspaper reporter in his story indirectly quotes someone to the effect that "One minute of motion picture (is) the equivalent of thirty minutes of talk." This story also includes a direct quote from John E. Burchard that "the idea which a reader derives from Ernest Hemingway's *The Old Man and the Sea* comes after the reader has absorbed some sixty thousand words. This takes at least an hour." The newspaper report concludes with the statement that, "Mr. Burchard ventures the opinion that a similar understanding could come after a few minutes study of a painting by a skillful artist."

It is quite possible that you could get just as superficial an understanding of Hemingway's book, "reading" at a thousand words per minute as you would from looking at a painting for a few minutes. However, these points of view are not to be argued with here. What is important is that a conscientious copywriter, an earnest headline writer, a responsible newspaper, a group of thoughtful and dedicated people all conspire, in spite of their own most cherished aims, in giving life to a monstrous notion which is the very opposite of their intentions. Pictures are not better than words except where the words are not understood or the "meaning" of the picture is clearer to the viewer than the words. Pictures are very effective for telling the *what* of things but rarely the *why* or *worth*. Where pictures begin to approach words in this function they lose their visual values in the same proportion as they gain in communicating ideas. But ideas sometimes shrink and harden from use and we make marks to stand for them. This is how alphabets are born and changed.

What has to be clearly understood is that there is no one sovereign way of getting information. Pictures are good. So are smells, yells and bellyaches. But information is the raw material of communication. Information isn't even that unless it is used or a use is contemplated for it. Communication is a social act. It is always concerned with other people. It can be done with a grunt, a bump or a glance. It can be rich with "meanings" or with feeling or with a mixture of both. The *what* of things can be reduced to the simple symbols of mathematics but the *why* and its *worth* needs the poets' magic and the shared remembrance of dreams and hopes. The crudest television commercial pays homage to this when the dancing bottles or marching cigarettes picket the screen with little signs, pleading for closer attention.

Words are slippery things. They won't stay put. They pick up meanings and colors not "intended" for them. They suffer or profit by the company they keep. In the mouth of one man the word "love" can be a plea. Other lips can make it a curse. Its meaning can be reduced to the equivalent of "like" or expanded to mean "worship." The word *red* may mean truth, beauty or falsehood. *Liberty* can become a dirty name; *chain* a term of endearment.

What happens to words can and does happen to any symbol. A flag, a statue or a city can "stand for" opposite things for different peoples. But we trust the words we share with others until we or they are misunderstood and even then we distrust them more than their words. We often have a very firm belief that the words that we use are the same as and as real as the things they stand for or the acts they represent. Languages are filled with reverent remarks like "I give you my word!" The tyranny of the two-letter word *is* forces us to act, sometimes as if the word we use for a thing is as real as the thing in itself. This causes us to misjudge the nature of the actual world. It worries us and even makes us sick. Some people in this world, not of course as civilized as we are, even think that it is dangerous to let anyone know their real names for fear that the name-knower would have power over them. But let any man call another a fool or a liar or question the social regularity of his parents' marital relations and he will act as violently as any other primitive.

We are a nation of loudmouths. We got that way on the tinker's trail and at the boasting parties around frontier campfires. We have more tall tales in our folklore than you can find in all of Europe. But our tallest tales have become merely conservative estimates of our actual performances. Pecos Bill rode a tornado. His great-grandchild rides a Thunderjet at ten times the speed. Paul Bunyan's Blue Ox would be worn out by a medium sized bulldozer and Johnny Inkslinger couldn't even feed the cards to an obsolete IBM bookkeeping machine.

We wallow in this flood of words, but it's of our own making. We've painted the clouds with ads for soap, curtained the country-side with billboards for baby foods, and crammed the general air with electronic declarations about the benefits of laxatives and deo-dorants. But the anxiety we should suffer in the face of this flood is only apparent in the warnings of the permanently disenchanted.

Of course it is true that the shell game is played on us everyday in the year by peddlars, purveyors and producers of everything that we need and use and a lot that we don't need, never wanted but cannot do without.

It is certainly true that our intelligences, however great or meager are insulted and conned by the anti-logic of the huckster but it is about time that someone blew the whistle on the anxious applicants for our intellectual guardianship. This is not to say that there should be no concern about the connivance of the wool-pullers and pharma-ceutical wolf-criers but, rather, that those individuals with off-center sensitivity over the sodden plasticity of the masses ought to learn to read their dials and counters with more accuracy and objectivity. The mass mind is a myth.

The mass media for communication, and we have invented and perfected all of them here, are effective upon the masses only so far as distribution of "information" is concerned. The only apparent mass movement that television has so far been able to effect is the concerted and collective use of plumbing during the commercials.

Mass action can still only be effected where there are masses. The motion picture could do this, but we lack the indecency of Hitler's Leni Reifensthal; besides, our whole population is never anxious about the same thing at the same time. We rarely suffer more than a few mob scenes during any year, and these are engineered by methods that were invented by the old Greeks and still require a man with leather lungs and a ruptured psyche.

No, we live splendidly and dangerously in this word ocean of ours. Its currents are strong. Its shoals are treacherous but it is not the whole of our environment. We inhale and exhale words for our social living, but we do this for purposes, to make or change things or keep them as they are. To do this we must take thought and to think we must be able to hold ideas still long enough to compare them. To make comparisons we must be able to choose and choice requires that we have preferences. None of these acts are possible if we cannot manage and master the words that we use. The mastery that we have gained is the measure of the cultural distance we have traveled from the cave. It is a long long way. We have negotiated it through our ability to make, read and act upon signs. Early man was a good sailor on the sea of life. We are navigators.

In the following sections of this book the sources of our skills will be examined. To do this we will have to see how words are born and how they die. We will need to know what changes man has made in his living since he learned how to freeze ideas onto a page and yet make them more alive. Then perhaps we can understand what is involved in the act we loosely call reading and what it means to initiate a child into its open mysteries.

2

The World of Words That
Makes Man Human

Man has always been trying to find out what he is. Aristotle said he was a political animal. The old church fathers said he was a religious animal. Some cynics say he is nothing but an animal. Some poets find him a little less than the angels and some suspect he is the maker of the gods. But whatever else he is, man talks. It is hard to know when he started talking, but it is certain that he has never shut up.

Von Fritsch experimented with insects and reported in his book, *Language of Bees,* that the bees have a very effective and complicated form of communication. In his excitement over his discoveries he calls it a "language." Animal psychologists have found that many animals have rudimentary forms of communication, by body movements, odors and cries. There are myths and fantastic tales of human beings learning the "language of the birds." Saint Francis and Siegfried were supposed to have had that skill. Some legends tell of humans living with wolves, baboons and the great apes and acquiring their "language." All of these tales are good for cold winter nights or technicolor movies.

All living organisms can be said to "communicate," at least with their own kind. Many can make their biological needs known. They can give and receive some warnings. They can indicate the presence of food or danger, or the opposite sex where one exists. They can communicate but they cannot converse.

23

To talk is to be able to communicate nonsense, to share laughter and the fear of things that never were. To talk is to be able to welcome someone else into one's own teeming brain, to share our yesterdays and to control the shape of tomorrow. Susanne Langer says:

Language is, without a doubt, the most momentous and at the same time the most mysterious product of the human mind. Between the clearest animal call of love or warning or anger, and a man's least, trivial *word*, there lies a whole day of Creation—or in a modern phrase, a whole chapter of evolution.[1]

We think with language. We breed ideas. We make noises that stand for things and marks that stand for the noises. With language we rehearse, we practice, we try out events before we attempt them in actual practice. We save ourselves from aches and pains and deaths by using words and signs for what we hope and plan and dare. By words we mold the squalling, squirming blob of *homo* and make it *sapiens*. This is what distinguishes us from the apes. Man talks to man and this distinguishes him from the animals. Through his talk and the memories of his experiences he has made his character and his personality as immortal as any living thing can ever be. We pummel and pound the ears and eyes of an infant with sound and actions until it responds in kind and we train and teach it to make our noises to declare its needs and demonstrate its awareness of us and the rest of the world about it.

We humans do this whatever our estate. There are no "imperfect," half-formed, budding languages. The "crudest" savage in the most undeveloped "preliterate" society possesses a language that is as "grammatical as Greek, and as fluent as French." [2] Even the so-called click language of the Hottentots is effective enough to deal with abstract notions of truth, goodness and beauty. Even the Stone Age Australian Bushman can deal with the mysteries of time and

[1] Susanne K. Langer, *Philosophy in a New Key,* New York: Mentor Books, 1948, p. 83.
[2] *Ibid.,* p. 84.

"togetherness." All languages sing about infinity and name surprises as soon as they occur.

Language is the product of many things and conditions, most of which are uniquely human. But to seek for origins of language has thus far been a fruitless affair. These things we do know: The human infant has a tendency to babble. This babbling is seized upon by all of the other humans past that stage as a source of interest, pleasure and excitement. The infant is talked at and very quickly gains the skill to make sounds which elicit responses from the talkers that are profitable. It gets attention. It gets care. It is taken into the club. The distinctly human attributes that foster the growth of language are then: (1) all human infants have a tendency to babble, to play with their vocalizing equipment; (2) humans live in remarkably stable groups; (3) these groups are characterized by a profound concern for the individual members. No other animal group, or "family," even remotely approaches the human family in this concern for stability. One of the main elements of language is that it is social at its base. Another element, which is not easy to discuss without some highly technical digressions, is that it reflects the ability of the human mind to abstract, to take out of an experience those aspects which that mind considers or decides are essential, and to then use what has been abstracted, to stand for, to symbolize that total act or experience. The main difference between animal noises and human sounds is that the noises are practical and concrete, the sounds are signifiers and are abstract. Consider the words "yellow" and "dog" and the myriad "meanings" that attach to them singly and together.

We saw earlier that "reading" refers to a wide variety of acts that a man engages in, in his several environments. All of this "reading" is accomplished in terms of his continually growing experience and his varying abilities to meet and manage that experience. Man lives in a space-time world which the animal cannot enter. Man is able, through the power of his symbolizing words to deal with time and place and condition in such a way that he can make yesterday and tomorrow haunt the present. He uses time as a string with which he ties events together in manageable packages. As he stabilizes these binding acts, the sounds he uses to mark them acquire *meanings* which are highly portable. They could, for example, be easily carried to the camp fire for examination and approval; something that couldn't be done with a mammoth or a thunderstorm.

Language; the social group, the babbling baby who learns the sounds, the time-holding acts that make society live and learn longer than any of its groups or members; language in words and motions, in pictures and attitudes, in pottery and priestly poses; language that makes the word a fact or a broken tooth precious and puts man at the still center of the turning universe. Language is the seed bed of miracles. It makes man human. It brings permanence to a changing world. Yet it too changes. Meanings rub against each other. Words are slurred and slipped into each other. Symbols rot and die as new ones are born in pain and work and glory. And all the while words are fed to babbling babies who learn them and use them to change the world as they change the word.

The words in a man's mouth have sometimes been revered, especially when that man was bigger or older or different from the rest. If this difference was wisdom and the group benefited, his words might live after him. If the difference was the dark power of mysteries, his personality might live after him. In either case language would seem more permanent than men, and so words might come to be respected above the acts of men. And men would protect the words and see to it that they were not "mis-spoken" or sullied by meaner tongues. Thus the language of the temple and the court became separated from the language of the people and myths might be raised to prevent the "proper" language from being mauled and molded by common use. Dedicated groups in temple, court or academy might make language an end in itself rather than the tool it must be if it is to live and grow with its users. The sixteenth-century French Academicians tried to stop the change of their language on dead center and only succeeded in separating themselves from the living language.

We may laugh at the sixteenth-century Frenchman's attempt to hold back the course of his living language yet even we today often repeat his mistakes. There is the tradition that makes "English" a special subject that all children must study in our schools. All too often this means that the living language is torn apart and mounted on paper and blackboard and examined for its "parts" as though it were an insect or a dried flower. Some teachers report that children like these exercises, knowing quite well that they are bored by the subject and usually turn, for the survival of their interests to the tricked-up form and the security of the routine.

Fortunately this abomination is not committed upon the very young child. It is the excellence of our teaching in the early years that makes it possible for so many of us to grow up to find such deep pleasure and use in the spoken and written word and survive the assaults of later education.

The child's introduction to language is usually a very pleasant one. As we have already seen, it begins as a tool for getting things done. It very quickly becomes the prime instrument for the management of the universe.

The first voice sounds that the child makes appear to be reactions to bodily discomfort, to hunger, pain and cold. The intelligent mother quickly learns to distinguish these calls for help from each other. In fact, by learning to identify them, she helps the baby to make each sound unique. Watch any newborn child and see how the sounds it utters are accompanied by diffuse and generalized movements of the whole body. It cannot yet separate one muscular movement from another. But it learns very quickly and in a matter of weeks is able to cry with a minimum of bodily gyrations.

Very soon the baby discovers that there is pleasure to be gotten just from the making of sounds and this is where the miracle really starts to work. The babbling and cooing noises begin and usually by the time the child is six months old it is able to make practically all of the sounds for fully articulate speech, plus a lot of sounds it will never need at all. The rest of the family automatically seizes upon this activity of the infant and feeds him language sounds almost as fast as food and for more sustained periods. It isn't surprising then, that an infant who has reached this babbling stage is able to reproduce the rhythmic pattern of the sentence of the language spoken by the family. Anyone possessing the delightful combination of a baby and a tape recorder can easily discover that the sentence rhythm of either or both parents and any other member of the family who regularly attempts to talk with the child will be reproduced by the baby in wonderful nonsense syllables which, even so, carry meanings.

About the same time that all this is going on the infant seems also to discover that it is able to express something of its own feelings and emotions. He does this in the simplest way we all employ; by varying the pitch, volume and frequency of the utterances. With these devices the baby soon has the whole household hopping. He can easily become a tyrant of the word. He very often does.

The birth of true language in the child is a product of the tireless care adults usually give to the infant in introducing it to the spoken word. If this kind of care were continued in all stages and phases of child-rearing, perhaps most of the psychological troubles that beset us would disappear. But, should a child be neglected at this stage, his chances of ever becoming a fully functioning human being diminish with fearful swiftness. There is very little direct evidence to go on, but from the few reports of children who have survived infancy without human companionship, we can see that they become creatures that resemble humans only roughly, in bodily contour. The so-called wolf-children are cases in point. Very few of them have been scientifically studied. None seem to be able to survive the "captivity" of human companionship. None seem to possess any kind of language whatsoever.

Without human companionship, without people to respond to his babbling, to be excited by his chattering, without a world of talk to enfold him, the wild child is only a wild creature and his psyche had best be left to theologians to ponder.

These are of course such extreme cases that they serve best as source material for Rudyard Kipling's Mowgli and Edgar Rice Burroughs' Tarzan. They do point a moral. The child is capable of learning greatly but it can suffer quick and permanent damage if it is not welcomed and warmed by continual human shelter and companionship. But for all that, the human infant is a rugged little creature. Ushered into the word-holocaust of our society it not only survives but thrives. Until a generation ago human voices wakened us to human faces and forms; today with the disembodied voices of radio and the flat, untouchable faces of television, the infant still is not disoriented, despite some of our past fears. True, today's child does not accord the same attention to the spoken word that his grandfather did, but that is not his fault. His father and his father's friends have so cheapened the value of the spoken word that almost none, least of all children, listen very carefully. But this is only true in those social deserts that are dominated by the Cyclops-eye of television and the funnel-mouth of radio, where the speech production, by flesh-and-blood, approachable humans, is reduced almost to the animal level of grunts for food and sexual attention.

Conversation requires the fallow fields of interest, enthusiasm and appetite for adventure. It requires a lust for ideas and the intellectual courage necessary for their acquisition and defense. The minds of children have these requirements and they hold on to them tenaciously until they are finally wrenched away by the thick-hided insensitivity of stultified adults.

This is not to be taken as descriptive only of some of the homes of the economically or intellectually underprivileged. These intellectual slums exist at all social levels, among the first families as well as among the late comers. A book-lined wall is no defense against this corrosion. College diplomas are poor shields. The life-giving talk that starts at the edge of the crib must continue and grow more brilliant and more exciting as childhood unfolds and youth arrives. Speech, the mind's tool, must be whetted on talk that is rough with the harsh bright crystals of wonder born of new experience. If the child would learn to read the meanings of his world, he must have acquired all kinds of skills in dealing with its multitudinous signs that hold that world together long enough for him to begin to learn to understand.

The experiments in sound that the child engages in during the first months of life are interesting and exciting to itself and to the adults around it but it is nothing like the great adventure that begins when the child produces its first word.

There is a lot of delightful nonsense about the first word. Parents will argue that the labial noises combined with vowel sounds *means* Mama or Papa depending on which parent is more anxious, aggressive and acquisitive. *Mama* usually wins out in most languages. Why shouldn't it. She hovers lovingly over her child, feeding it cues and grasping at even remotely familiar sounds. The child, being intelligent, of course catches on. After all he does want to become a member of the club and this giant creature seems to be offering easy initiation. It makes the noise *mama*. She is transported; she caresses, feeds and fondles the child who immediately senses the positive quality of this wondrous emotion. That the child may use the noise *mama* rather indiscriminately for a little while is overlooked. By dint of high-pressure teaching it finally attaches the "word" to the "proper" object.

Mama is the word that so often comes first in the child's vocabulary in most languages for two complimentary and cooperative reasons: it is made up of sounds that are produced easily and early, and, Mama is around to see that it does so. In some cultures and languages, *mama* loses out by a shade to other imperatives. Some Puerto Ricans insist that the child learns *aqua* first, for the simple reason that it "knows" how precious and scarce water is.

The great infant discovery in language is that words control things even when the thing is as great and as powerful as *Mama*. When it produces another sound, in our culture it may often be a word like *ball,* the infant is on its life-long way to control of the universe. For the infant, the word *ball* becomes a word-sentence. It can have many meanings depending on the way it is produced. It can mean, "there is a ball," "that is a ball," "I want the ball," "where is the ball?" and so on. With the word-sentence language becomes a tool. And learning the use of this tool is an accomplishment greater than all other learning.

After the first word, the rest is easy, or it appears so. Yet the infant has been learning the wonder of words for a long time before it begins to apply its knowledge. For words are understood long before the power to utter them develops. The words that come first may look like names, they are in fact really action words. A quick examination of the "ball" sentences above demonstrates this. These grammatical terms are scientific counters by which sophisticated adults organize their knowledge about language, after the fact. Some investigators insist however that "the quickness with which an infant grasps the possibility of expressing the idea of change, desired or resented, by the addition of a verb (or some part of it) to a noun is usually an indication of the quality of his intelligence." [3]

The awareness of change is the great marker of awakening to the nature of the world about us. For the child it is the beginning of time. It is the way the world starts spinning. It makes possible the mental "seeing" of here and there, then and now. When the infant knows change, life-in-motion really begins. This is the time when the greatest word care is, and rightly must be, lavished on the child. Objects must be shown to it, and actions demonstrated and the words attached thereto. It is a wonderful play time for the parents and the child. It is the great learning time, if the child is healthy and the environment rich in joyous occasions. But it is a time of danger too. The word causes the thing to be produced. It is easy to begin by thinking that the word and thing are inseparable and then to act as if the word itself were the thing. This is a dangerous disease from which too many of us suffer most of our lives. Consider how violently we sometimes react to words themselves. Think of the last argument you had. Remember how you hurt and were hurt by words. But the child is insulated from this by ignorance, by lack of experience. In the early months of its life it responds to a stimulus outside its body much as an electric bell responds to its button being pushed.

Children don't invent words, at least not in the beginning. They

---

[3] A. F. Watts, *The Language and Mental Development of Children.* London: D. C. Heath, 1944, pp. 37–38.

might get in the habit of saying *ba-ba* right after a bath or a feeding or some other pleasant affair. Perhaps the mother has made it a practice of giving him a ball at this time every day. Mama may seize upon this sound and decide that "he wants his ball." She gives it to him and then gets into the habit of associating the sound the child makes with his "wanting" the ball. If she forgets the ball one day and he continues to cry *ba-ba* she will say, "He is asking for his ball." And at this point she is probably right since her "asking" or "wanting" something is probably only a more complicated way of responding to a similar situation. The infant has now made another giant step forward in his management of his language and his world. Bloomfield calls it abstract or displaced speech in which the infant names things even when they are not present.

Actions are perfected by their results and so it is with speech. As he gains skill in making the sound for *ball*, he is understood. He gets what he wants. He is satisfied. And the polishing process continues. Parents and older children constantly feed him cues for more effective language usage. He learns. They are delighted. His wants are met more readily. He eagerly matriculates in the school of human speech. The curriculum is complicated but never boring. He receives the best teaching he will ever get and in fact all other teaching he experiences will be measured against this in terms of satisfaction and effectiveness.

All this is prologue. Mind is now in high gear. *Homo* is joined for life to *sapiens,* and the human being truly has been born. Now he can rehearse things that never were and ask, "Why not?" Now he can proceed to catalogue the universe of things and acts and conditions. He begins to learn to plan, which means he begins to learn to select from what he *thinks* are possible outcomes of what he proposes to do. He *takes,* literally handles, thought as he has learned to handle things, and his reading of the charts and dials of life become more and more precise.

This is the kind of reading that the schools in our society eagerly wait to teach him. This is why the women in the children's garden teach their charges the wonderful game of "show-and-tell." For all his learning has been with the wholes of his experience. The after-learning, much like the after-burner in a jet engine, gives after-power to his ideas. This after-power is his ability to abstract, to take the mind sign for *ball* and measure it against *orange* and see differences; to take the shock of recognition of these differences not as a hurt but as an opportunity to find out more about things and their relationships. He has learned the whole sound for ball, the whole picture for ball, now he learns the whole printed "word" for ball. It will still be a long time before it is worth his while, and his skill in abstracting is equal to the task of taking the word apart in sounds and signs and putting it back together the way it was.

By the time the child arrives at school for the first time, he has acquired a huge operating vocabulary. Dr. Mary K. Smith, in her study of the vocabularies of public school children estimated in 1941, that this was about 24,000 words. Today, after more than a decade of the mass use of television, this estimate must be revised upwards by many percent. These are the resources the child brings to the learning of reading. He is, by any count immensely skilled in the basic uses of his language.

As Robert H. Seashore pointed out (*The Packet,* Vol. 2, No. 2, November 1947), "Most of our common beliefs about vocabulary size are grossly in error and practically always are underestimates of our actually measured attainments." For example, starting with the basic 24,000 in grade one, vocabulary growth continues at an average of about 5,000 new words per year until at grade twelve we have about 80,000. And it doesn't stop there! There is plenty of evidence that vocabulary continues to expand throughout life.

Notions about vocabulary size, even among teachers, are heavily encrusted with myth and nonsense. Ways of counting vocabulary go from the supine to the ridiculous as for example an early English "study" made by Dean Farrar, who lay on his back one afternoon, listening to fruit pickers talking. At the end of his musings he *guessed* that they didn't use more than a hundred words apiece!

Seashore noted several of the sources of misinformation about vocabulary size. Some researchers have counted up the number of different words used by great writers and have totaled their findings, as if they were grocery lists. Thus; Shakespeare is accused of 15,000, Milton of a paltry 11,000 while the loquacious Frenchman, Hugo, was found to use 20,000. A high school student can see the holes in this "argument." Skillful writers, in their writing try to employ the simplest and most appropriate words from a list of approximate synonyms. The list taken merely shows what the writer used in his writing, not at all *what* he knows. There are words that can only be found in completely unabridged dictionaries which nevertheless are known by significant numbers of children in the first grade.

The high priests of the written and spoken word in New York and Hollywood and points in between who have accepted and defended the myth of the average American's twelve-year-old level of mental development have been short-changing themselves and their parishioners for lo, these many years. Small wonder that there is rarely richness and texture in words that they put into the mouths of their characters on screen, radio and television or in the advertising sermons they compose on the virtues of the products they peddle. Any but the most inept story writer, poet or novelist, who at least begins by loving his language, can and does produce sentences, which by comparison, are deathless prose.

What does this mean too, for those hack-writers of childrens' stories, and the publisher who stables them, who don't know or cannot understand the enormous appetite that children have for the acquisition of new words and the new ideas they represent? Children, almost all children, read and enjoy books and magazines that are not crippled and restricted by some fond adult's silly and ignorant notion of "appropriate children's language at the correct level." And don't let these dwarfers defend themselves by claims that "children like the simplified version." The first commandment of the advertisers' decalogue is "Make 'em like it." They have followed that injunction to the letter, as they have also followed the Dark-Ages psychology of the behaviorists who practically invented the scare-'em-and-sell-'em school of advertising.

This is not to be taken as a blanket indictment of the total produce of all our mass media. It would be bootless and querulous to follow the argument further, except for the fact that even with the poor materials they offer, our children today learn and use more words and ideas even faster than we did in our childhood. This age of ours shouts up a greater storm of words than even the Periclean Greeks who were able to talk the stone ears off statues. We are every bit as excited and intoxicated by words as were the Elizabethans although we still suffer in the ankle-length skirts of Victorian prissiness.

The youngest school child who has had years of continuous happy language experiences comes to school literally in love with the words in his mouth. If he is lucky, and in the elementary schools, he may well be, he will find teachers who respect and share his joy and his treasure. They will join him in his adventures. They will read with and to him. For them, the storyteller's carpet is still in flying condition. Not until the children meet their first disenchanted quasi-grammarian for whom sentences crawl on their "parts of speech" will they sober down to boredom and drudgery. Not until then will they discover what they probably suspected, that words can bite and sting and even kill.

3

The Magic of Words That Frighten
and Sustain Him

When the baby begins to cruise the world in his crib he discovers magic. He has only to scream the word *mama* into the fastness of the night and Mama will materialize, full-blown and real. He has only to pronounce the word for *water* and she fetches it from beyond the darkness. He has only to say *'fraid* and she melts his fears in her arms.

Malinowski, the anthropologist, says that magic is the institutionalized expression of human optimism, of constructive hopes overcoming doubts and pessimism. Magic, he says always appears in an organized way whenever and wherever man finds that he can't run things by any practical means. He thinks that magic has been good in organizing early experience and in inspiring hope and confidence in the individual.[1]

John Dewey objects. He said that magic obstructs intelligent study of operative conditions and wastes human desire and effort in futilities. He claims that magic is found whenever someone seeks to get something for nothing.[2] Yet Charles Morris goes between them when he points out that the use of magical formulae in a given culture may give greater confidence to those who use it in carrying out specific tasks, and so increase the effectiveness of the work they

[1] Irving, J. Lee, Editor, *The Language of Wisdom and Folly,* New York: Harper and Brothers, 1949, p. 242.
[2] John Dewey, *Human Nature and Conduct,* New York: Modern Library, 1930, p. 26.

do. Magic here has the elements of those symbolic acts out of which moral and religious values may develop.[3] Someone else observed that magic is merely toddling science, the premises might be wrong but the desired ends are accomplished for undiscovered reasons.

Magic starts where language starts, with the notion of a sign or a symbol that stands for a thing or a condition. And the two are wedded when infantile remembrances of the efficacy of words call forth pleas and prayers. If things work out as well or as badly as desired, word-magic is born. But the seed of word magic is planted in the crib. It is nurtured when infant thinking is short-circuited into believing the word is an aspect of the thing-in-itself, when he is taught to be frightened or pleased by words alone. This is what prevents him from generalizing, from abstracting, from thinking itself. It prepares him for the uncritical acceptance of stereotypes, those short-hand terms for all of our most complex feelings and attitudes about man and nature.

Stereotypes are the most persistent form of word-magic we treasure. They are the direct opposites of the cataloguing activity of the thinking mind. They grow where minds are tired and confused. They make it easy for us to separate "them" from "us." They take the drudgery out of thinking. They remove all shadows. Things all have their "right" names. Things are right or wrong, good or bad, themselves or their opposites.

There is an attribute that some words seem to have, which the child learns very early. They carry social charges with the power to shock. The first one the child learns might be "naughty" or "baad" or "ah-ah" or "shame." Whatever the word, he gets the shock and a recognition of the awesome power of these words. But when he tries one of them out he might find that it backfires. He may discover that he has used a "wrong" word, a "dirty" word, or at any rate, a dangerous word.

The abstracting power of language makes it a marvelous instrument for dealing with new and strange experiences. You can take

---

[3] Charles Morris, *Signs, Language and Behavior*, Englewood Cliffs, N. J.: Prentice-Hall, 1946, p. 243.

something that never happened to you before and, by finding elements in the situation that are even remotely similar to what you know and remember, arrive at a kind of understanding that makes it possible for you to survive the event. This is the way an atomic explosion becomes a mushroom, a warm breeze becomes a kiss, an automobile may snarl or purr or whine, and stars can smile.

Words may be likened to growing pearls. They too, start with a kind of irritation, an itch to name, an ache to symbolize. They are valued for their color, their "perfection," their clarity. But words words have a way of acquiring values other than those ascribed to them. Even as the child learns them they can become "good" or "bad." They can be powerful, or gentle or somber or sweet. And as they become these "things" they get another kind of life. They can stand for other words which stand for other ideas which finally refer to some concrete act or thing.

"Mother" is such a word. Psychologists may have something to say about some of the consequences arising out of the child's effort to transfer the meaning of *mama* with its easy sounds, to the difficult *th* sound of *mother,* and the considerable social pressure involved in the formalizing of the word. But *mother* is good and kind and powerful; the source of sustenance and wisdom and security. The goodness of mother as a personality transfers to the word itself and so, onto any word attached to or modified by it. Thus; motherhood, mother-love, mother-lode, mother-land, mother tongue, mother church, mother wit and Mother of God. The idea of "mother" and experience with "mother" has today been put to use in the market place to peddle everything from pills to candy and Cadillacs. In this function the "good word" serves to short-circuit any critical thinking about the subject to which it is attached.

The power of this word is so great that even a group of critical graduate students in a seminar devoted to the study of language has great difficulty in separating their own "good" experience with mother, from an objective discussion of the effect of such a word in non-motherly contexts. They might admit that some mothers are not what they "should be," but theirs are. They might agree that the word has been used for partisan, parochial and even economic ends—but they will insist it is a "good" word. And so the school must once again take up its task of the teaching of reading, for these people have lost the ability of discriminating between the precise "meaning" of a specific word in a specific context, and their own various and sometimes conflicting experiences with the word sound and objects to which it has referred.

Words wear down with the corrosive effects of social use. A word like "naughty" which once was a powerful imprecation now is more appropriate as a diminutive term of endearment. A sacred name like Jesus Christ is mauled, for magical safety, into "cripes" or "jiminy cricket." A great oath like "By His Wounds" degenerates into "Zounds!" and dies amid childish laughter in the comics. But words today can suffer more rapid wear in the shining colors of ad writers' palettes. Hollywood and Madison Avenue have hamstrung the power of all adjectives even to the superlative degree. A product is never merely good, it is "better than ever!" A film is not merely excellent. It retreats into the womb of time to become "The greatest epic of the century!" The nadir was reached a few years ago when a film was introduced with full page ads in full-sized newspapers with the signal declaration that "Words cannot describe . . ." and some artwork of a heap of discarded dictionaries mimed the film's merit. The wordless ad ran for several days until the next crowning achievement of cinematic art cowardly retreated behind a curtain of words and the old formula of the "century's greatest . . ."

What this at once bespeaks is the general virility of language and the poverty of the copy writer's pen, a result of malnutrition at the schoolboy's desk and the home library. It tells too, of the lack, both of respect and of forbearance of the antics of the thinking mind as it wrestles with the facts of the universe, as it attempts to order the conflicting experiences that make life the challenge that makes us human.

Writers of "teenage books" and simplifiers of the "classics" for teenage readers are in unconscious league against the children. The so-called career books which, while attempting to perform a neces-sary function, that of introducing the high school youth to the world of work, do so in such a standardized format, with such stock characters and pat situations that both story line and educative mes-sage are lost in a rubble of words. Mary wants to be a photographer for a screen magazine. She begins at the "bottom" and like the perennial Horatio Alger hero, slowly by surely achieves greatness, security and a hint, but only the slightest hint of possible love. No real challenges beset her. She meets paper dolls, not people. Her goals and her values are shadows of the screen world. The young readers have strong stomachs. They gag a little, read the stuff, and shrug it off.

There is a great need for books that carry messages to our youth but need they be, in format and in style as dishonest and as tawdry as the worst aspects of the world they represent? Isn't it possible to have flesh-and-blood characters, faced with recognizable problems win through the achievable goals or fail in an instructive way?

We must return to this theme later but a word must be said about the "classics." What the screen has done to Ulysses and the Trojan War needs no retelling here, but the vulgarization and bowdleriza-tion of those two great stories can best be summed up in this "trans-lation" of the meeting between Ulysses and his son, which was found in a school textbook. Telemachus says, "Hi, Dad!" The comics are more honest than this. I doubt that Homer is appropriate read-ing below the junior year in high school, but if it is brought in at all, it should retain some of the meaty flavor of the original.

The child, and the man too, of any age is ready to experiment with ideas, ready to test their competing claims of any degree. This readiness is at once foolhardy and fabulous. But in our world, and most especially in this country, we most respect the truth that can be tested publicly. The greatest contribution that American thinking has made to science and philosophy is the argument from Missouri: "Let's see you do it!"

Hucksters who huddle behind your typewriter barricades, beware! Do you know that the children are watching? They see cheap and shoddy "demonstrations" of a product's "excellence." An immaculate hand wraps apples in the tissues and dips them in water. The unidentified competitor always comes out second best—until Junior retreats to the kitchen laboratory where he discovers and reports— "Any paper napkin will hold together in a pan of water so long as you don't touch it to the bottom." The consumers research reports of these young, unsolicited investigators would jaundice the eye of the most sanguine television director. "Warm water will make all pills dissolve faster." "I can make a colored solution clear up with my home chemistry set." "I timed my father shaving with that razor—he doesn't have a tough beard and it takes him three minutes." "I tried the hidden brand cigarette test on a dozen people and no one could tell what they were smoking." "You can't see pink toothbrush when the toothpaste is pink." "Deodorizers just make it so you can't smell the stink!"

These children are brave warriors in the battle for the protection of the provisional truth. What a crime we commit when we league ourselves with the printed devils and the electronic "wizards" to defeat them. The children beg for a chance to sharpen the weapons of their wits with family argument. They start when they discover the awesome power of the "why" question and we beat them down at the barricades of adult *ennui* and indifference. They continue the struggle up through the 'teens, as they seek through the power of words to solve the riddles of the world. But teachers and parents team up and shove busy-work at them. Discussion is deferred until inquiry dies and peace or discipline returns to the room.

One of the basic jobs of the school, of all modern education is to help the child and the young adult make of his language, not a barrier to understanding but a highroad to knowledge and the management of experience. Not only must he be taught to "read" the signs of his world as they confront him in ever increasing orders of complexity; he must have the ever-renewing opportunity to learn by mistakes and successes, how to think through problems to useful solutions, how to accept these solutions—for the time being—until better ones come along, how to know better ones when he sees or makes them, how not to be dismayed or thwarted by the dark magic of the twisted word.

This kind of teaching begins in the early school years, soon after the basic "sight" vocabulary is acquired. Children are taught that meaning is more than the sum of the meanings of the words in a sentence. They get practice in learning how to discriminate among possible meanings and to choose the one that is most appropriate for the particular sentence being read. New words are readily added to the vocabulary but meanings are added even more rapidly. The rate of this addition is a direct product of the total language experience of the child at home, in the school, and in the community.

Home, school and society at large have carried on this kind of instruction throughout most of our organized history. At one time it was thought that the mind needed "training," the soul, "bridling" and the body "developing." That time is still present in some dark quarters of pedagogy. Yet it was an honest enough notion, despite its psychological ignorance. It was concerned with the full development of the whole child, but only one "faculty" at a time. It started from the premise that we had at birth all the "mind" we would ever get, that all the mental skills we would ever need were all there, requiring only to be "awakened." It thought of the mind as possessing specific faculties that needed only to be exercised and trained.

What we say learning is will determine how we teach. What we conceive learning to be will depend on what we think *mind* is. Thus if the mind is merely a collection of faculties, training is required. The puppy and the child can go to the same school. But if mind is a function, as most contemporary psychologists would insist, then learning is a far more complex affair. Yet it starts quite simply. As we have already seen, the newborn infant can do three things very well. It can cry, it can kick and it can suck. It does these from the very first moment of independent motion. This is its first and simplest learning but all its other learnings will be built upon this simple structure. It responds in a certain way to something outside of its body. It is "aware of its response" and what happens as a consequence of that response, though not in any clear or precise way.

There are many different kinds of learning. But the distinctly human kind begins with the great discovery of error, of failure. "The first failure," says Walter, "is the beginning of the first lesson; learning begins with failure." [4] The uniquely human talent is that we can "domesticate error." In a sense, this view of learning is rather like the so-called feedback principle that is so useful in electronics and the source of so much controversy in group dynamics.

The "birth of error" is in fact the beginning of wisdom. You can only be aware of error when you have attempted to act on an interpretation of some symbol and have been frustrated. You ask "why" and begin to search out the "reasons." You check through the file cards of your memory for similar experiences. You rehearse past outcomes. You estimate the possible consequences of a proposed course of action and then you act. Wrong again! And the learning continues.

This can be and often is a painful process and man is always seeking ways of minimizing or circumventing pain. This may be called the principle of least human effort. For, besides wishing to avoid pain, man seeks to avoid spending more energy than is needed for any activity. This too, is another source of thinking. Rehearse the battle in the wardroom. Find your failures in the blueprint stage. Try out a working model! Practice! Make sure! Calculate the risk!

The gamble, the guess and the hunch are peculiarly human weapons in our struggle with our several environments. We have developed them in our attempts to reduce the element of chance that looms so large in the universe as we try to understand it. So long as we accept things as they are, and ask no foolish questions the world stays small and we are safe. Once we begin to seek explanations, once we dare to trace out the development of events, the unaccountable occurs, the accident appears, the puzzle arises. We are confounded into contemplation. We stake the assets of our experience and our intelligence on the turn of Nature's card. If we

[4] W. Grey Walter, *The Living Brain*, New York: W. W. Norton, 1953, p. 138.

have "read" her correctly, we win another round. But more than that, we win a blue chip of *information*. We know a little more about the way the world spins. The puzzle is a little less puzzling and though the world becomes larger we are not lost.

Along with the principle of least human effort there is an urge towards security and certainty. The Horus myth still haunts us. We want to be sure. But we want the knowledge without the work. We lift the cup of magic. It spills words. Echoes of ancient hopes and anxieties surround us. Sacred and unutterable names of the good gods and evil forces, cryptic names of strange animals and far places, alchemical incantations and the soundless symbols designed to plumb the unknowable depths—words and signs that stand between us and all that is hostile, challenging and confusing. It is pleasantly exciting to remember this from our modern oases of central heating, flush toilets and electric lights. It is a measure of our gains beyond the pyre, the dungeon and the hovel. It is the height we stand on above the mindless superstition of yesterday. Our modern words are good, clean servants. Are they?

In the late 1950's, in Tokyo, a group of worshipers at a national shrine panicked when a wall collapsed. Someone screamed a word and the worshipers became a killer-mob, mangling itself. In another part of the world, two good citizens told a little boy with a darker skin, that he had learned bad things. He confirmed their complaint by the words he used. They killed him.

Any day a group of sober senators will shout angrily at each other when one of their member utters a phrase like "self-serving." Everyday, people listen, not to the words spoken by others, but only for a chance to start talking themselves. Words are good servants when they merely point to things like "Men's Room" and "Ladies' Lounge." They become destroying demons when they label us "Red," "Fascist," "Infidel," "American." It comes as a great shock to us sometimes when we discover that a name or title we respect to the point of reverence can be used by other people almost as a curse. We have often and successfully used abrasive terms for the Japanese, the German, the English, the Russian, but to see the word

"Yank" used as a dirty name, after all we've done for the starving ingrates makes our patriotic blood boil.

Languages are made up of words and parts of words that label things and acts and qualities. Words can "explain" things. They can also explain other words. Whenever explaining is done, it is satisfactory if it makes possible some kind of directed thinking, thinking that has purpose. Teachers have toiled through the centuries to impress upon their students the necessity and the duty to "complete the thought." But the artist in man learns that some words tell more when they say less. Sometimes an "unfinished" sentence opens up more ideas while a completed sentence stops all speculation. Hints can reach beyond the horizon of meaning. Word fragments can suggest otherwise unimaginable worlds.

> There was a young fellow of old
> Who spoke of a wonderful town,
> Built on a lake of gold,
> With many a barge and raft
> Afloat in the cooling sun
> And lutes upon the lake,
> Played by such courtesans . . .
> The sight was enough to take
> The reason out of a man's
> Brain; and to leave him daft,
> Babbling of lutes and fans.[5]

Oliver St. John Gogerty leaves things loose and unfinished—but his words' meanings go on weaving the tapestry of the senses long after the sound stops.

You can play such wonderful games with words, especially when you leave *sense* out. "Ibbity–bibity–sab"—"eeny–meeny–miney–mo" —"onery, uery, ickory Ann"—"harvey, jarvey, jig, jig, jig." Language has bounce and sweep and rhythm to it. It runs past simple meaning and children quickly see its poetic possibilities. All the

---

[5] From "O Boys! O Boys!" by Oliver St. John Gogarty in *The Collected Poems of Oliver St. John Gogarty* published 1954 by The Devin-Adair Company, New York. Copyright 1954 by Oliver St. John Gogarty. Reprinted by permission of The Devin-Adair Company.

games they play are rich with it. They love the measured sound of stamping feet and thumping drum. They tap pencils all through high school, driving teachers mad. They wallow in the unsubtle rhythm of "Rock-an'-Roll." They accentuate the positive. The downbeat is their signature. But the inadequate teachers rally—and the kids hate poetry before the boys' voices change.

A syllabus now in use in a metropolitan school system directed that the child "memorize thirty lines of poetry during the school year." The teacher is urged to instruct them in the "basic poetic form," to help them distinguish between metaphor, simile and analogy! Some of the poems offered in the accredited texts bear little relation to the possible experiences of the urban child. How can a child whose knowledge of hay stacks is confined to the yellow colored illustrations in a basal reader make any sense out of Carl Sandburg's reference to "pearl grey hay mows"? The rural child suffers too, of course. How can a child of the plains who has seen no canyon and no skyscraper get the imaged reference to lower Manhattan? The only solution lies in the teacher's patient guidance by definition and discussion to lay the groundwork for useful vicarious experience. It is a chore too often neglected in the press of "learning the poem."

Poetry is not to be experienced, it is to be studied. Its sudden splendor is quenched in written exercises. The canned lessons at the end of each section of the class reader compound the felony. The questions asked are often inane. The "activities" suggested are even worse. It would seem as though everyone is conspiring against the child and the poem.

The spark remains. It is fanned by the singing commercial, but dies horribly amid the cant and chant of the shouting huckster. All the "good" things he felt about language are turned against the child. Repetition of sound now destroys sense—uncompleted sentences now shackle thought—metaphor now shimmers in a deodorant's mist and analogy languishes at the bottom of a dishpan. The words are tarnished with detergent grey.

The magic of the word that holds the universe still so that we may learn to use both word and universe, is also the magic that puts the same butterflies in our stomachs whether we see a snake or hear the word. The thing frightens us—the word frightens us; therefore word and thing are the "same"—not really so, but magically so. And we react often as violently to such words as the most primitive man who ever lived.

The semanticists have struggled diligently and at times brilliantly against this and associated diseases of words and word users, no more brilliantly however than Gilbert and Sullivan who warned, "Things are seldom as they seem; skim milk masquerades as cream." "Semantics," according to Hayakawa, "is the study of human interaction through the mechanism of linguistic communication." [6] Some practicing semanticists go so far as to claim that their "science" alone can bring about human sanity. They even propose a therapy based entirely upon semantic orientation. They erect an imposing semi-private terminology including such omnibus words as "psychophysiological," "multi-ordinal," "many-valued," "neuro-semantic-relaxation," "etc.", and so forth. They are wholesome toilers in humanity's vineyard who would be quick to point out that the way I write these words is itself "loaded, colored and clouded." That they claim too much for the awful power of the word, as their negative critics insist, is probably true, but they bring a wide-eyed and at times naive clarity to the whole problem of man's struggle to understand himself and his world. The teaching of language and its usages, which is based upon this "semantic orientation" is the healthiest antidote we have yet devised against infections from diseased words.

For many years now, at least since the early 1940's, most teachers of teachers, especially in the Language Arts (we used to call them English teachers, but then they acted like teachers of English), together with the National Council of Teachers of English, have sought to educate into the profession, people who would have respect for the words in everyman's mouth. It is not a very easy job. Teachers are usually made out of very ordinary people, just like us.

---

[6] S. I. Hayakawa, *Language in Thought and Action,* New York: Harcourt Brace, 1949, p. v.

They come with their own prejudices which they protect as diligently as we do. They are often as resistant to the lures and challenges of education as the rest of us. For many of them, teaching is "just a job." They do as much as they are told and no more. They often go into the profession under the mistaken notion that it provides something called "security" which they suspect is a goal in life. It turns out to be a very low hurdle. They get over it and settle into the useless anonymity of the tenure trap—now before all the teachers' professional organizations—and they are as many as there are blades of grass—take common cause against and rip these words out of their bleeding context I hasten to add that I am talking NOT about ALL teachers, or even MOST—only a sizeable minority in a profession where even ONE dullard is a danger to our commonwealth.

We have survived and will continue to survive, as a nation, despite quack doctors, cheap-jack lawyers, self-serving clergymen, dishonest accountants, venal engineers and half-informed scientists—we have survived because the overwhelming majority of these professions are honest, ethical and deeply committed to a life of service to their fellows. Even when they don't say so.

4

The Mark of the Book That Sets a Man
Off from His Unlettered Fellows

Many an anthropologist working his way through the brush of some back country is surprised to find that the natives are not surprised by his arrival. Their own wireless communication may have preceded him by days. Although they may have no permanent writing, no system of regular signs, they will have developed codes for acoustic or visual transmission of information that is every bit as efficient, for their culture, as the high-speed telegraphic symbols are for us. Their reading of the impressions on each other of the world about them will be remarkably sophisticated. They will be able to deal with abstract ideas and generalizations of a rather high order even though their writing might be only twisted fibers or broken sticks. Even this simple cultural development, however, will be in the hands of priests, the initial developers of any writing in any culture. The spread of information and the elaboration of the means whereby it is spread are the result of two parallel efforts; a rationalistic purposeful desire, and a religious impetus, as Julius Lips points out in *The Origin of Things*.[1]

The exchange of information about practical matters probably began, as it still begins in school, by the "show-and-tell" method. Rehearsal, mimicry and imitation are the channels for simple learnings. Walking, talking and play are learned this way. The development of muscular skills begins this way too. Much of the education

[1] Julius E. Lips, *The Origin of Things*, New York: A. A. Wyn, 1947, p. 242.

49

of children in the so-called non-literate societies is also of this nature. The use of tools, the care of the body, of the home, these too
are learned in this way. It is the thinking about practical things that
first confronts us with problems of choice. It is out of choosing that
the really "big" problems of life come upon us. For choice involves
preference and preference, after infancy has to have the support of
"reasons" and reasons need powerful sanctions if they are to be called
"good" or "better" or "worthwhile."

This is where the religious impetus shows itself. While the rest
of the group is providing food and shelter and the other necessary
protections, the priests are "keeping the books," doing the tribal
accounting and "reading." They have the reasons, the explanations,
which they will make available to all who need them, for an appropriate fee. That fee is part of the birth dues for the continuance of
the race. That fee, like all other fees that man pays to man, is his
index of the division of labor. When man begins to specialize, he
begins to civilize. The hunter no longer makes his weapons. The
weapon maker no longer gathers the flints and sticks. The gatherer
has no time to hunt, and the women only have time to prepare the
food. Specialization fractures the personality even as it increases social efficiency. It needs another specialist to see the whole group as
a unit, and put personality back together. He is the shaman, the
priest, the reader of signs, the generalizer, the teller of tales, the
guardian and weaver of tradition.

There are three great, revolutionary inventions that have brought
man from the level of animality to his present estate: speech, writing
and printing. Speech made man human, writing (even the most
ancient cave paintings are writings) made culture and continuity
and history; printing liberated the power of the public mind and
made possible all that we have and are.

A history of articulate language can best be written by poets with
the aid of social psychologists and anthropologists. Without a time
machine we will never find its birth. The history of writing is available to any school child. It is a fascinating story that starts at the
verge of prehistory, perhaps in those Aurignacian cave paintings,

probably thousands of years earlier. It moves slowly as the pictures become picture writing, as the pictures are formalized into simpler outlines, as the outlines are reduced to easily managed characters. Then it moves rapidly, in the global time scale a matter of half a dozen millennia, until the characters are further simplified and reduced in number to about two dozen, which in combination are capable of representing most of the sounds man can make or cares to make. Every home library should have in addition to the Bible and the telephone directory one of those delightful children's picture-book histories of the alphabet. The genealogy they demonstrate is expurgated, usually including only the Egyptian, Phoenician, Chaldean, Greek and Roman characters with occasional excursions into some demotic scripts, the so-called writing of the common people. Inadequate though they may be, they can serve to give both child and parent some respect for the depth, dignity and ancient lineage of the written word.

There was no great systematizing inventor of writing but there was a class of inventors, the priests. In all of the high cultures they played an enormously effective role in the development and perfection of their societies' respective scripts. The knowledge that they gained and transmitted, of the art of writing, the skill with which they could use it to transcribe the spoken word, the almost-magic with which they could preserve forever and with accuracy, the memories and legends and great doings of their people, all this meant power; political, social, moral power that spells authority and control. With this power, one of the great ages of man began. The laws, customs, traditions, rites and creeds that were formally committed to memory and tediously passed on from dying elder to younger leaders created the literary heritage that built dynasties and countries and finally cities. This wealth was mainly for the uncommon man. The mass of his fellows dragged the Stone Age behind them well into the Golden Age of Greece. As Nietzsche remarked of the uncommon man, "What have they whereof they are proud? Culture, they call it. It distinguishes them from the goatherd." It did. It still does. But only in the dark corners of the world, for the third revolution, coming at the dawn of technology released the pent-up wisdom and information of the ages and created modern man.

The printing press was a cultural time-bomb. Printing provided a medium for the broadcasting of thought and thought, even once broadcast in this manner, cannot ever again be completely suppressed. The hand-wrought manu-script, laboriously copied, limited severely in circulation, vastly expensive, could be available only to the lettered few. The printed book was the beginning of a system of literary irrigation. It nourished almost all it touched. It destroyed the old private channels of privileged thought. It made literacy endemic in the land. The radical challenges of the copied manuscript could effect only palace rebellions. But no censorship can or ever could completely suppress the message of the printed book. It was this new power, as Briffault says and not the revival of ancient literature or the rebirth of classical learning, that was mainly responsible for the Renaissance, or—as it is more accurately called— "the Awakening." The stirrings and inquiries, the curiosities of the savants, all of these would have at best produced another tiny Golden Age such as Periclean Greece or the Arabian Caliphate. But the book, wedded to the languages of the people had a kind of fly-wheel effect whose momentum increased with each generation.

The alphabet had been available for two thousand years, but paper and ink and the pressure of a screw created the first true mass medium of communication which finally made the common man uncommon. Despite the valiant last stand of the defenders of large truths and private powers, despite all the laws and acts designed to prevent the serf "from learning letters," learn them he did, with clerical help where he could find it, with only the book and a few rumors and rudiments, if he could not.

With printing, knowledge became public, but this didn't happen with the first press-run. In the beginning, printing was considered to be essentially a way of avoiding the copyist's mistakes. The mass-production aspect of the enterprise was quickly recognized when cities all over France and Italy followed Gutenberg's lead and set up presses. While the first books were religious texts they were followed in a very few years by editions of the classical literatures of Greece and Rome and grammars of those languages. Before 1469 presses began to operate in Milan and Venice. In 1471 a press opened in Florence and Politan wailed that "now the most stupid ideas can in a moment be transferred into a thousand volumes and spread abroad." [2] Copyists, suffering the pangs of technological unemployment railed against the new gadget and swore that no good would come of it. But new skills were needed. Type setters and pressmen appeared, as did machine designers and artists of type faces. The machine, as usual, bred more jobs than it destroyed.

The early printers were devoted to scholarship. Some spent their lives and fortunes in gathering and editing texts and in turning out fine yet inexpensive editions only to see them pirated hardly before the ink was dry. But they wrought so well that neither plague, nor famines, nor war could ever again obliterate the treasuries of man's knowledge which they had built.

The leaders of the Reformation, however, were the first people to make any significant use of printing to make knowledge and information public. They were anxious to extend the influence of their doctrines beyond the ranks of the scholars and the princes and into the ranks of the common man. And so religion once again was securely wedded to writing but this time the marriage was public and plebeian. As Carter observed; "In the whole long history of the advance of printing from its beginnings in China down to the twentieth century, there is scarcely a language or a country where the first printing done has not been either from the sacred scriptures or from the sacred art of one of the world's three great missionary religions." [3] Pope Alexander VI immediately recognized the profoundly disruptive effect that printing would have upon existing institutions, and in 1501 he issued his edict against all unlicensed printing. Even before this, certain German universities established

[2] Will Durant, *The Renaissance,* New York: Simon and Schuster, 1953, p. 315.
[3] T. F. Carter, *The Invention of Printing in China,* New York: Columbia University Press, 1931, p. 17.

censorship boards. Gutenberg had set in motion a tide as powerful as the one King Canute failed to stop. The printing press had liberated the public mind, made popular education inevitable and eventual political democracy inescapable. In one sense printing is and has been the ultimate weapon. Handbills, broadsides and pamphlets have wrecked the ancient regimes and new documents, secular, yet humanly sacred, announced the coming of each brave new world. It is a noble effort that spells out the Rights of Man: wholesale publishing of the statement creates a public goal which the public will achieve. The hand of the censor is too small, too weak and in the long run too unskilled to halt the roll of the presses. For those who have suffered censorship this statement may seem naive but the printed pages that have flooded the world give testimony here. In the fifteenth century there were perhaps 30,000 printed items in all of Europe. By the middle of the twentieth century that number had grown to more than 17,000,000 titles. In the United States alone, in the year 1927, over 470,000,000 copies of books and pamphlets were printed. In 1955 the total was close to 800,000,000. In 1963, books alone probably accounted for more than a billion and a half!

The prevention of literacy has a long and dishonorable history. The good philosopher Plato was one of the earliest to suggest ways of inoculating the masses against reading. He suggested scaring the daylights out of them. The *Index Librorum Prohibitorum* has since 1559 listed the works the Roman Catholic Church prohibits. The Index has a certain parochial efficiency, but it suffers, if that is the proper word, as do all such lists in that it serves more to popularize the books it censors than to prevent their being read. Almost all organized religions have tried with varying short-term success to censor the reading habits of their communicants. Protestants of all persuasions have been as thorough and even more violent than the Catholics. We have suffered book burnings from the time of Anaxagoras, in 450 B.C., down to the most recent conflagration of offensive comic books, and we will undoubtedly find fuel for fools again this year, who will be persuaded that their conception of Truth is more accurate than their less perceptive fellows. By this they can mean that the other people are less educated, less articulate, less moneyed or simply that they are not members of the right clubs.

A person in the throes of learning can be a thrilling sight. It can also be frightening if that learning is going to equip him with the ability to ask embarrassing questions. The serf of Merrie England who got his letters might discover that the laws could be used to protect as well as to abuse him. The returning Negro G.I., who came back home after having been contaminated with literacy during the Second World War, might have to be killed to get such nonsense as individual legal rights out of his head. It is always unsettling to have private information become available to the public. Don't we adults sometimes have to spell out words so the little ones may be appropriately hoodwinked? The young, the pure of heart and the uninitiate so often have a simple faith in knowledge. If something has been written down and printed in a newspaper or a book, they believe that it was put there to be understood and if necessary, to be acted upon. The sophisticate is impatient with such nonsense. There are, after all, fictions to be maintained, even as Plato suggested. Mere literacy is no defence against him. He has become persuaded that the real nature of Truth is known completely only by him and his kind. He believes that he alone reads rightly and others are dupes and dullards. He is in his way a kind of inverted censor who in the very act of "protecting" the right of free inquiry is desperately anxious to direct it into what he deems are "appropriate" channels.

If you, the reader have been following the preceding paragraph uncritically you have probably assumed that you and I would be in agreement about the meanings of such words and phrases as *serf, returning Negro G.I., child, uninitiate, Truth* and *sophisticate.* Now you are trying to examine them more closely. Now you suspect a trap. Words once called into question unleash more questions. You may begin to resent the words, and the author too. Words like these have multiple meanings and their contexts cannot always narrow them down to one meaning.

Many years ago Heywood Broun wrote a delightful little fantasy called *Gandle Follows His Nose,* in which an apprentice sorcerer accidentally liberated a standard lamp genie who offers the usual services. Gandle requests and receives such necessaries as castles and grounds, hunting and livestock stables, suitably stocked, money and the other useful treasures. When he then demands "the fairest and most virtuous lady in the land" the supply of miracles stops. The genie tells him that it is an easy matter to move castles, trees, treasure and animals from elsewhere to here, but that "words are slippery things . . . they won't stay still" even when you can manage to get hold of them. This comes as quite a shock to a bright boy who has had considerable experience with magic words only to discover that apparently ordinary words are not as easy to control. This is the perennial lesson in word-reading. This is the earliest and continuing reason for the existence of schools.

As the areas of public knowledge become more and more extensive, more and more words are needed to manage the new information. We are constantly making new words out of the scraps of old ones. We "cannibalize" (a new meaning for an old technical term added to Anglo-American vocabularies during World War II) both dead and living languages for them and produce such words as "thermometer," "assassinate," "automation," "punch" (from the Hindi *panch* meaning five, hence a drink with five ingredients!). Margaret Schlauch's book, *The Gift of Tongues,* has several fascinating chapters on the care and breeding of such words. The point to be emphasized here is that we expand our vocabularies to explain the things we do and that the very act of explanation itself extends the word lists further.

The wonderful power of abstraction that a child in our culture so readily acquires with the use of the common noun, is a device for word economy that some so-called underdeveloped languages do not have. After having had experience with only a very few dogs or cats, the child is able to apply the words accurately to other canines and felines. Some languages require specific words for "black-cat-in-a-dark-alley," "black-cat-on-a-fence-in-the-moonlight," "my-black-cat-on-the-rug," etc. The marvelous power of our common nouns to work with the interchangeable parts of modifying words make it easy for us to localize and specify any experience. This is not meant as belittling to other more cumbersome languages. Whatever the language he uses, man can and does express the most complex ideas and activities he engages in. He does it with greater efficiency and subtlety when his social and technical literatures are developed. But whatever the subtlety, however great his proficiency, whatever his language, he can be victimized and confused by the slippery word. He needs the protection that only skillful instruction in the art of purposeful thinking can provide. This protection cannot be bought like a ready-made suit; in fact, that metaphor doesn't even approximate the problem of description. This protection is rather like a lifetime endowment policy, one that continuously changes as the needs of the person do. It begins, as we have seen, with birth and the social introduction of the child into the world of words. The parents are the initial underwriters, and while they may hold an equity in his development far into adulthood, they enter an insurance pool with community, school, church and finally the wider society. (Again, notice consciously the kind of reading you have just done to "get" the idea enclosed in this metaphor.)

We have, in the sketchiest of ways, been examining the history of reading and writing and have only implied how by reading and writing, man rose from a low estate to the management and control of what William James in a wonderful phrase called the "whole blooming buzzing universe." This is high romance and great adventure, far more than can be encompassed in a book, much less a single chapter. To awaken this sense of adventure, to keep it alive and ever-growing, this is the responsibility of all to each. It is most especially the responsibility of the adult and the mature to the young and inexperienced. That is why we insist that it is one of the major purposes of the school to introduce the child to the record of our management, the story of our adventure and the wealth of his heritage.

It is more than a crime of omission that this is not so in most schools. Our record of performance in the child's garden and the early grades is generally impressive. There are more excellent teachers to be found here than anywhere else in the world of schools. Although deterioration is a harsh word, it has a pungent accuracy in describing the classroom as we go up the educational ladder. At the college level the performance often descends into the abysmal. It is indicative that we refer to college teachers as lecturers, instructors and professors. Again a mollifying word of caution to the misreaders; if you had fortunate or wonderful college experiences, congratulations! Please bridle your rampant generalization. What we are concerned with here is the brutally insensitive and efficient misteaching that makes poetry dull, literature a chore, science an agony and "social studies" a bromide.

Schools are better than ever, just like the movies, but look at what they are better than. What I have to say here might properly be damned as the snarlings of a snob, but consider the materials available and used in the schools, especially the secondary schools; consider the textbooks. Even the name is beginning to frighten some publishers, and so—in this age of packaging miracles—new labels and formats are created. This has proven effective for shortening and cigarettes, but those products were effective to begin with.

The very notion of a "textbook" harkens back to the days of the uncritical worship of the written word. It goes back to the company of scholars and their mentor, to exhaustive explanation and interpretation of the *word* and to the ritual worship of that word. Understanding then was measured in the quantity of regurgitated "facts," in the slavish reiteration of the revered passage. So long as we are concerned with the maintenance of ritual, there can be no complaint, but education is another matter.

Examine a modern textbook on "social studies," a label that educators invented for the quite legitimate identification of those sciences concerned with human affairs in order to avoid the destructive distillation of the record of human enterprise into refined and unrelatable subject matters of history, economics, civics and industrial, social, political and physical geography. It was a noble endeavor but it degenerated into a potpourri of unidentifiable origins. The modern social studies textbook is the coagulation of this mess. It is usually so big and so heavy that the small child (and they come quite tiny in the seventh grade) has difficulty just carrying it. It is usually printed in double columns and occasionally shows up in three! It is chock-full of photographs and sketches of widely varying vintages on which reproduction restrictions are small or non-existent. It usually begins its story with a descent into the mists of pre-history. Now this could be exciting, but the seventh grader, for example, "has had it." Early in his first year in school, his teacher probably showed some wonderful pictures of cave paintings and of mammoths and dinosaurs and of Cro-Magnon and Neanderthal men. Later the same kind of material was given to him again, and now in junior high school he is getting it both from the science teacher and the social studies teacher. How long can he remain polite?

But my complaint is not so much with the material as with its manner of presentation. Most textbooks are written by amateur writers (in the worst meaning of the phrase) or by literary hacks (ditto) whose knowledge of the child's mind is inadequate, obsolete or non-existent. They write "down" to the child. They use a simplified vocabulary and denature its contents, and if the book is "graded" for "easy reading" for the "slow-learner" the felony is compounded. "Terence, this is stupid stuff!" Worst of all is the bastardization of history. The dawn of conscience is strange and unfamiliar territory from which the writer flees in quick paragraphs along the safe shores of the Tigris-Euphrates, and thence to the warm banks of the Nile. Here they begin the "teaching" of history by stereotype. Babylon had hanging gardens and Egyptian artists could only paint in profile. Oh, it is true that the books cull some scraps of information about something called "social life," but it is diluted with snippets of story and lame fictions. We meet a little Greek girl who takes us to the Stoa. Little Timon tells us what SPQR stands for on the pedestals of first century Roman statues. These digressions get in the way of the flow of facts, poor though they may be.

This device is used even more cavalierly in sections dealing with the modern world. "Let us take a plane and fly along the African shores of the Mediterranean Sea." The child reads this in a classroom in Brooklyn. There is no objection to stories as such, providing they are legitimate stories, worth reading for their story value. As they are invariably used in the textbooks, they serve mainly to strangle what interest survives.

The social studies textbook suffers from trying to do too many different things, for trying in fact to present a kind of compendium, a unified concept of the whole human enterprise. The writers (and we often have teams as large as those who gang up on television and motion picture stories) are just not up to such a job nor are the children capable of dealing with such a concept were it properly presented. The organizing of such diverse yet related knowledge is one of the larger purposes of the whole of our educational effort. The curriculum designers, when they are skillful and intelligent keep this in mind as they program the twelve-year school experience for the child.

The indictments of the social studies books can be applied with slightly varying emphasis to the other school books. The science books, for example, should from the very beginning keep the child aware of the unity of all science, for without this unity, unlike social studies, the scientific enterprise becomes a boring and meaningless jumble of ill-assorted facts, which, incidentally, accounts for the widespread ignorance among both lay and professional people about the nature of the universe. Physics is generally reduced to a brand of Newtonian mechanics; biology (beware of sex) is a cross between the cook book and puppy-raising; chemistry is a compound of tricks and kitchen piddling; and astronomy is a silly chore that gets mixed up with the English teacher's unit on Greek mythology.

The shame of our schools is that science is, in spite of all its recent seductive improvements of curricular presentation, so generally disliked. The crisis in science education does not spring, as has been claimed, from the raids that industry has made upon our school staffs, but rather from the fact that science has been made so terribly unattractive to the child. It is true that the best scientific minds do not stay in the schools, but a good scientist is not, by virtue of his competence, a good teacher; offering the service of army officers or industrial research men to the schools will not resolve the dilemma and, if anything, will aggravate it. A good teacher is not merely a person with a deep knowledge and love of a subject, but one who has an excellent understanding of basic principles, a love of people and children in particular, an ability to awaken and maintain interests, to direct those interests towards successful experiences and above all to foster wonder, curiosity, patience and an appetite for understanding. Brilliance in teaching is an acquired skill and it is not necessarily spectacular. It grows readily when the teacher has access to good materials.

The complaint is often made that many teachers are not very intelligent, that for generations the schools of education have been getting the leftovers of the liberal arts and engineering colleges; that teachers are status hungry, security-minded (in the economic sense) and timid in most other respects. This is a blanket indictment, which, considering the many disabilities under which the profession labors, is far less true than it might be. There are more good teachers than poor ones by any standard, and this is about as much as we can say of any of the professions.

This digression is necessary in order to emphasize one other aspect of the textbook problem. Since ex-teachers have a hand in the making of these books, and sometimes they have been among the most successful members of the profession, they tend to incorporate "teaching aids" in the books. The result is sometimes pretty horrible. A lesson, or a collection of lessons that has proven effective for one teacher sometime, somewhere is not likely to be effective everywhere. One of the sources of its excellence is that it was originally tailor-made for a specific group of children living in a certain place at a certain time. When these lessons are immortalized between hard covers, they become strait jackets for other teachers. When these lessons are shredded into bits called study helps or "questions" they often cause intellectual indigestion in the reader. The argument for these lesson plans (usually published separately as teacher's manuals) is that "teachers aren't very bright." Perhaps we have already touched that argument—but a crutch has never been very good as a polishing instrument.

The effect upon children is nowhere more painfully demonstrated than in the Language Arts books. In the upper grades the "reader" becomes an anthology, often euphemistically labeled Adventures in Something or Treasure of Something or Something About Living. There is a lot of good writing between these covers, along with the usual leaven of "stupid stuff." If the child should by any chance find enjoyment in what he reads he is disabused when he turns the last page of the story to find "Something to Think About," "Something to Do," etc., and usually the teacher wants him to think and do what the book says. Even if she didn't, that page of contrition would be there warning him to suffer for his joy. Nowhere in the anthology is this more grievous than in the poetry sections. Imagine having the guts of a poem laid bare—having to search for precise meanings in the wonderfully ambiguous province of the singing word! Imagine having to sober up so quickly from such a delicious image-binge! We are allies in a war against children's enjoyment of poetry. The love they have is different from ours, if we love it at all. They are uncritical of anything but sham; they are worshipful of image and sound, of texture and rhythm, and we feed them a diet of indigestible labels and fatty interpretations.

The anthology wreaks as much havoc on the story. It tears the soul out and labels its squirming parts. It asks questions, cunningly devised to short-circuit anything but the "appropriate" response. It provides "busywork" instead of a springboard for further high adventure. Sometimes a piece of "literature" or "classic" writing is gratuitously peppered with footnotes which are often misleading, often inaccurate, always certain to stop the reading eye when it should be surging forward with the swell of the author's style.

There is only one kind of anthology that I am prepared to accept for any subject. It hasn't been made yet. It is a kind of wish-book, a mail-order catalogue saying simply, "Boys and girls, here are some samples of what some people thought and felt strongly enough about, to put into this form, and good enough to have printed. Read them, and if you like any of them, the publisher has provided whole books full of each kind. You be the judge. You buy." Then both teacher and pupil would be free to range as far afield as their wit, energy and imagination could carry them. No strait jackets, plenty of help, intellectual and emotional wealth for them, cash on the barrelhead for the writers, editors and publishers.

If you detect a hint of crass materialism in the foregoing, I have been too subtle. For far too long the publishers have had a captive market. It has not been without competition but it has been of a sickly sort. Worse, it has neglected one of the fundamental functions of good merchandising, that of the development of future and diversified markets. Very few of the children who have been exposed to the textbooks, will, because of that exposure, be inclined to become book consumers. As an industry, textbook publishing is really sick. It sells almost one third less books now than it did in the thirties. In part this is the result of competition of other kinds of materials, audio-visual aids in particular. In part, however, it is caused by the unnecessarily long life of the product. Kids can be destructive but it takes the efforts of dozens of them years to use up physically a book that has already died educationally. There is no logical reason why most textbooks—if not expensively illustrated—cannot be made completely expendable, why each child should not literally own a copy which he can actually use, mark up, underscore and make margin notes in. These are reading skills he cannot develop too soon. They can be the source of real pride of ownership. They can help him learn how to own books. This can make the industry healthy, expanding and far more enterprising than it has been in a generation.

One of the major concerns of this book is with the expansion of a reading public. In this chapter it has been concerned to show that reading still "maketh the full man." But whatever the schools may do, however excellent the product of the publishers become, unless the family as a whole nurtures an interest in reading, unless books have an important place in the home, our greatest efforts will be poorly rewarded. The younger generation of parents can be reached by an intelligent campaign of advertising and taught the importance of assuming their obligations towards the development of their children's reading skills and appetites. For it cannot be emphasized too sharply or too often that the mark of the book is a friendly mark and that reading has its deserved status for the bulwark that it is to the free mind, the haven that it offers to the puzzled spirit. With the book a man can be alone with his thinking, feeling, growing self. In the book, the author is always patient, willing to say over and over again what he has said once. The book can never be circumscribed by the tyranny of an electronic clock. A growing shelf of books can be at once a barricade against despair and a ladder to a full and useful life.

5

The Value of the Book
in a Changing World

Change is our earliest teacher, our constant companion, our dearest enemy, our most fickle friend. Change spins the multicolored top of the probable world and it becomes the shimmering mist of the possible universe. Change is motion and light and fear. Change is the standard and the thing it measures. Change makes telling worthwhile and listening useful. Change is the what and the why of reading.

If words are slippery, so is life, so is living. One of the first aspects of this world that we become aware of is that most things just don't stay put and since we have already come to rely on the basic regularities of existence, this is quite a shock. At first this is of small consequence, resulting in those early gentle failures that create error and make learning possible. But the evidence piles up rapidly and we are in the throes of the old Greek argument about permanence and change. Heraclitus insisted that all things change, everything is in motion, "You can't step in the same river twice." Parmenides said no, things just *are*, Existence is all, change is an illusion. Then Zeno, Parmenides' most vocal disciple, invented his paradoxes: that of the race between the loafing Achilles and the lumbering persistent tortoise, and that of the flying arrow. The arrow *appears* to be in motion but to be somewhere it must be at a certain point. If it is at that point it cannot be in motion. A flight made up of an infinite series of rests is unthinkable, therefore . . . . As for the race,

Achilles apparently overtakes the tortoise, travels half the distance and rests, then repeats the act for the remaining half of the distance. But no matter how close he comes to the goal, he will always have half the distance still ahead of him, therefore . . . .

It took twenty-two centuries for logic and mathematics to resolve those puzzlers, and they are still good for an argument among children and the uninformed. The solutions of these paradoxes require a conception of a universe in motion, *the doctrine of the continuum* as it is called, which eliminates discreetness and divisibility from the notion of extension and makes it possible for us to talk sense about the reports of our senses. Space, time and motion are literally all of a piece. We locate things and happenings by using all three as coordinates. We can hold things still only by suspending our attention about one of them. A process of selection, which is fundamental to all of the kinds of reading we have been talking about, always involves withdrawing our attention from a large number of things and concentrating it upon a smaller number. This is the way we see things. This is how understanding proceeds. This is also a source of confusion and fear.

In a world where no thing is certain, where all things change, change is sometimes frightening. Man must devise some way of holding things still long enough to permit examination and the growth of understanding. For any practical local purposes, certain kinds of change can be at least temporarily ignored. The slow erosion of the mountains, the even slower changes in the position of the fixed stars, these need not be considered by the shepherd or the navigator. When things are written down they are in fact pinned down. It is the written record, the printed page that holds things still long enough for them to be examined. Sometimes this function of the book is not readily apparent. It may be behind the laboratory instruments, behind the cameras, projectors, television screens and computers, but in the final analysis, these instruments are created by man so that he can more accurately read the record of what others have done before him; so that he may "try out on paper" older schemes and new ideas; so that he can keep the record straight.

When man invented history he liberated change. The old man had always complained that it was different in his day. Now he could prove it—more, if he had acquired a great enough reputation for wisdom and magic, he could use the sacred writings in the struggle to keep things as they were. The task was unequal in both directions. If he won, he could stop growth on dead center. If he lost, the center would explode and he, with all that he represented, would be lost. When the writing grew great on cave wall and temple, when papyrus scrolls were stacked like cordwood, and the writings were old enough to be ancient, they acquired a new kind of life that was immortal. They brought comfort and certainty, they clustered about the "thickening center of the turning world." They made measurement possible and judgment became a useful tool of long range thought. Whether we read the Egyptian Book of the Dead or the sere novels of our waning youth time stops for a while and for a while change is defeated. Like a wondrous insect it can be fixed upon the point of a book. It can be examined until fear of the unknown or the unmanageable is replaced by the comfort of knowledge or the joy of understanding.

We ask the schools to teach the beginnings of this wonderful skill and they have always complied with all their capacities. But until recent times our instructions have been precise to the point of strait jacketing the teaching enterprise. The tyranny of the three R's, which by the very name bespeak a truncated anti-intellectualism, acted as a brake upon the expansion of both the theory and the practice of education. Verbal facility and the management of symbols even within an academic framework are not in themselves guarantors of freedom to grow, to inquire and experiment. The atmosphere of the classroom and the attitude of the schoolman both worked against such ends. Evidence of learning was a cut above the ritual chant. Measurement of learning was by the quantity of regurgitated material. Children were to be trained just as puppies and pear trees. "Spare the rod . . . ." "As the twig is bent . . . ." the whole decalogue of such injunctions declaimed and employed within the confines of dark, spare rooms of American education in the early days of the nineteenth century.

For more than a century before the American Revolutionary War, Europe had been stirring with the notions of men who were concerned with improving the ways in which youth was educated. Johann Amos Comenius (1592–1670) wrote the first textbook ever to use pictures as an aid of understanding. He deplored the fact that in his day it was still common practice to teach physics by reading Aristotle. Start with the senses and with sense experience, he urged. Hadn't the Englishman Locke shown that the mind was a recording instrument for the reports of the senses? Etienne Condillac (1715–1780) went further in his condemnation of mere memorization when he wrote, "I grant that the education which cultivates the memory only may make prodigies, and that it has done so; but these prodigies last only during the time of infancy . . . . He who knows only by heart, knows nothing . . . ." His better known countryman Jean-Jacques Rousseau went still further, insisting that true education consisted more in doing than in merely knowing about things. He said that if the child be given the desire to learn, why then almost any method of instruction will be suitable. Along with the urge of interest the child must have freedom to seek and to express himself. And finally, something that echoes through all subsequent writings on scientifically oriented education, the child must learn through the natural consequences of his own actions. Above all, take things easy, he warned. The object of childhood education is "not to gain time but to lose it." "Hold childhood in reverence, and do not be in a hurry to judge it for good or ill . . . . Give nature time to work before you take over her business, lest you interfere with her dealings."

From the time that the lifelines of social culture were lengthened through the use of written symbols, deliberate education employed the social shortcuts of secondhand experience by the printed word rather than in the participated act, younger generations were forced to commit to memory those literary aspects of their heritage without always knowing what they were all about. This watered-down remembrance of things past is weak stuff, said Pestalozzi (1746–1827). "If a third person knows something and then puts his words in my mouth, which he has used to make his ideas known to others equally well educated, it doesn't follow that I understand anything at all of what he is writing about." Some teachers and many writers of children's books forget that injunction every time they face a child. Pestalozzi wanted the child to begin, where he had already been successful, in naming things. Once he did that, he could study the object named, compare and discuss its several qualities and attributes. Then, and only then could he proceed to the abstraction of its general qualities and so on to the definition of the thing. Summarize the teaching of everything through form, language and number. Of course all this puts quite a burden on the teacher. The time honored methods of recitation and regurgitation, with the book as the final arbiter of right and wrong, protected the teacher from strange and challenging questions. Pestalozzi wanted the child and the teacher out in the open. The lesson must be loosely structured. The teacher should be capable of following the interest of the child. This meant that the teacher had to be educated *and* intelligent, a rare if valuable combination. The structure of Pestalozzi's lesson, from object to definition eventually was embalmed in textbooks. It worked well for a long time.

There were, however, some very bad features to Pestalozzi's method of instruction, especially in the hands of unoriginal thinkers. Children could, and have been introduced to reading by learning the alphabet first, then proceeding to the mouthing and the making of syllables, thence to words. Words were added up into phrases, words and phrases multiplied into sentences. The simpler, more efficient way of beginning with whole words, was thrown overboard and some people are still trying to keep them off the deep end.

Both Comenius and Pestalozzi were concerned to get the child to have a clear understanding of the meanings of words. Their methods tied verbalization to conceptualization and both to the operation and reports of the senses. But this is only the beginning of learning. Concepts have to be tied together in more meaningful packets. New concepts have to be grown from older ones. Johann Friedrich Hebart (1776–1841), a German psychologist insisted that the child's past experiences help to condition and direct his reception and use of new impressions. Hebart had something to say about the way learning should proceed. His five steps were immortalized, in textbooks, of course. They were and still are the classic analysis of exposition. The lawyer, the judge, the salesman or the teacher will use them to explain a position, a product or an idea: They are: (1) *Preparation,* what do you need to get the idea across. This means research and study. (2) *Presentation,* tell them what you're going to talk about. (3) *Association,* tie it in to what they already know. Use familiar instances. (4) *Systematization,* give them other examples, show how they are connected. Give them the generalization, cite cases. (5) *Application,* show them how to use the new idea or gadget, give them problems to solve or work to do with the new tool. The teacher calls it homework, the salesman calls it a sale.

This is a good way to teach anything, even the television hacks know that, but for effective education, the child must want to learn. Educators call it motivation. Hebart said that the self-starting self interest of children must be appropriately directed by the teacher. Teachers, he said, usually try to interest the pupil in learning what they have to offer. Many still do. Hebart said turn-about is more accurate, pedagogically and psychologically. The children should learn so that they may be interested in learning more later. Children are complicated little creatures, with many and diverse interests. Channel them, but don't try to restrain the child in an activity unless you have something to offer that he can recognize as better. If you must inhibit him, be sure to give him something to do which you know you can show to be a useful activity. This still makes good sense.

Friedrich Froebel (1782–1852), a German philosopher, was even more insistent than either Rousseau or Pestalozzi that the child be more a guide than guided. He broke with the Calvinistic notion that play was sinful nonsense and insisted it was the natural posture of the child. Parents and teachers should be protectors not preventors of nature's laws of self-expression. To this end he invented the Kindergarten, the child's garden, filled with "gifts," the toys of learning. The infant toys we still buy are direct descendants of these "gifts." Froebel saw that play itself was educational. Play is the way by which a teacher may release the "hidden powers" of the child. Play can do this because it is the "natural" way the child expresses himself when not restrained by adults. Therefore, provide an atmosphere of play and the child will develop the freedom necessary for intellectual and social growth. Freedom, according to Froebel, was not a gift any teacher could bestow, nor could it even be given by God himself. Freedom was a quality of behavior that had to be achieved by self-activity. The Germans of this day, both bureaucratic and autocratic, wouldn't buy such notions. The democratic Americans did. It was the refugee Germans who came to this country after the 1848 revolution who brought Froebel's ideas both of theory and practice to this country. These ideas were first put into practice in the creation of kindergartens, one of the most wonderful developments in the whole history of education. Here the child was sovereign, treasured and respected. Here, too, began in an organized way the observation of child behavior which led to our modern careful concern with child development as the primary guide in the teaching of children.

Through the thought of all of these men runs the thread of the romantic revolution that had been coursing through European thought for more than a century. The classic mood, which they reacted against, was an expression of the fear of change. It had sought and received the support of science, politics and art. Its world view was one of order, regularity, a drive to perfection, a rule of law and reason. It echoes Parmenides in its search for unity and the security of stasis. Its concern was with the very largest aspects of life. Its accent was upon the ultimate worth of society, the abiding truths, the universal verities. It conceived of the universe as a perfect crystal sphere enclosing a miraculously precise clockwork. It saw God as the watchmaker-mathematician, par excellence. It sought to legislate change out of existence. But it just didn't work.

Life was not neat and order perceived was, so the romantic claimed, the ordering act of the perceiving mind. The romantic might be as fearful of change as his classicist contemporary but he had an older and a more courageous view of the role of the individual. There was the true sovereign in the forests of the world. He looked, as Matthew Arnold did, and saw that

> . . . the world, which seems
> To lie before us like a land of dreams
> So various, so beautiful, so new,
> Hath really neither joy, nor love, nor light,
> Nor certitude, nor peace, nor help for pain;
> And we are here as on darkling plain
> Swept with confused alarms of struggle and flight,
> Where ignorant armies clash by night.
>
> ("Dover Beach")

and yet he was really unafraid. This was Don Juan, Faust, Prometheus even, who saw the errant symbols of an uncertain world and decided that anything more than temporary order was death. Man was a making animal, the consuming creator, the merchant-artist whose hall-mark was individual freedom, whose goal was the evening sun, or the midnight tempest or personal death and social immortality. This romantic temper persisted and colored every other attitude, whether it was the idea of inevitable progress, the concept of evolutionary development or implacable determinism. It affected every activity, education more than anything else.

The idea of self-expression and self-activity as the keys to appropriate ways of teaching coupled with a profound commitment to *freedom,* as the only appropriate atmosphere within which the child could develop, approached, in the early days of this century, the dimensions of a cult. To teachers, so committed, progressive education—for they pre-empted the label—made the freedom of the child not only the major goal of education, but also its only proper method of instruction. This resulted in some peculiar practices which have been caricatured and pilloried for more than a quarter of a century. Freedom, ill-defined or not defined at all, became license. Anything that the child wanted to do, he was not only permitted to do but urged into. Respect for the child went so far that, if it were to converse in rich Anglo-Saxon monosyllables and even spit in the teacher's face, it was applauded for "expressing an opinion." This kind of well-meaning stupidity was born of a wide ranging ignorance of psychology, sociology and simple adult responsibility. That the child so exposed survived as a whole person is a tribute to the toughness of the human psyche. Fortunately this cultism flourished and faded rather quickly under the pressure of the honest toughminded ideas of John Dewey, who—surprisingly—in the public mind is often associated with these worst aspects of his own misapplied and misunderstood psychology.

Dewey's ideas on education stem from a belief that the teacher's method should make use of the social, psychological and biological propensities of the child. But he insisted that the idea of child activity be cued into means for helping the child clarify his own understanding of the meaning of and reasons for the schoolwork he is doing. Dewey accepted the notion of Froebel's "gifts" and Pestalozzi's "objects," but he warned that it is wrong to assume that objects must first be known before they can be used. The very process of using involves knowing. Knowledge isn't something that grows up in the head alone. To learn, to find out, to discover, one uses the whole body in a real environment. One learns about things by doing something with them or having something happen to oneself in the process of this doing. After the experience, it is time to talk. Dewey said that ". . . five minutes of unprejudiced observation of the way in which a child gains knowledge would have sufficed to overthrow the notion that he is passively engaged in receiving impressions of isolated, ready-made qualities of sound, color, hardness." The child is a restless, striving, reaching creature who seeks, as man has always sought, to manipulate things, not in order to learn any underlying principle but to know what could be done to and with them. The old idea to "Teach things rather than words" is good but not good enough. Teach them, said Dewey the meaning of things, the management of things and how they work.

Dewey published a wonderful little book in 1910 called *How We Think,* not to be confused with the rash of do-it-yourself volumes that flood the stores today. There are five steps in thinking, Dewey says: (1) *Knowing,* which in this book is another way of saying *reading;* knowing begins with an itch, a confusion, a difficulty. (2) *Locating* it, naming it, defining it, at least holding it still long enough to think about doing something to it. (3) When you think you have figured out what it is that is bothering you, taking some sensible *action* toward setting things right, so that you can go on doing what you were doing. (4) Thinking about what will happen if you do as you propose, drawing on your experience, rehearsing, giving it a dry run—"if I do this, then that will happen"—in short, making a hypothesis. (5) Actually trying it out. If you have thought well and accurately—no more itch, no more problem; if not, you check back at any rate. You have learned something, so you correct for error and try again. That's all there is to it—and it is a great deal. This is the essential of scientific method. But there is one more step implied in number 5—what we today would call the feedback principle—what we finally learn reconstructs all we know about the itch. Next time the itch is not merely a problem. It is a signal for action. We have learned a little better to manage the world in motion. Change is still with us but we now can read its direction and speed. Change is not a hint of approaching catastrophe, it is a challenge and an opportunity to live a larger life.

Our theme must be repeated here: the value of a book in the changing world is in its ability to hold things still long enough for them to be understood, until fear and confusion can be replaced by something less paralyzing. The book can make yesterday's seven thousand years a golden tapestry for the hero's hall. With it we can measure today's dilemma against yesterday's defeats. It may not diminish the press of our anguish, nor tarnish the glow of our achievements but it can show us connections, it can give us perspectives. How many times has man recorded that his world had gone to pot, had in fact ended with a bang or a whimper, as the case may be. The ancient Athenian, after the Greek World War, saw desolation extending into emptiness and yet Alexander came a few days later. The Babylonian father wept on his clay tablets that the younger generation wasn't a chip off the old block but those juvenile delinquents built the hanging gardens. The fat Roman saw the barbarians tear the heart out of his world but those vulgar characters carried the seeds of Dante and Da Vinci in their loins. And while Boccaccio was singing the swan song to delight, the cathedral builders were climbing to the skies.

Through the centuries, the school has sought to meet the challenge of change and in so doing has itself been changed in character, in scope and in its goals. Its basic function, however, has been to provide an area of constancy within which the growing mind and body of the young may be meshed in with the ongoing currents of society. It has tried to extend the securities offered by the family into the larger world. Sometimes it has mis-read its instructions and when it has done so, in any of its parts, these parts have perished. Sometimes it has been accused, both rightly and wrongly, of accelerating change, but when it has done so, it has been responding to the temper of the other institutions in society. In modern society, most especially in the United States, as schools have become professionalized the teachers have brought to bear on the problems of education as much scientific competence as they could garner from all pertinent fields of inquiry. For the most part this has been a healthy and a health-giving attitude. A good teacher today is not one who has merely mastered a subject, although this is still essential. He must know the facts of young life, of child development. He must know as much as is possible of the nature of learning. He must know how children behave in groups at different ages. His own life experiences must be continuously broadening. He must be steeped in his culture in both the esthetic and anthropological senses. If he specializes in anything it must be in generalizing, for the nub of the teaching process is in connecting the unique experiences in the classroom with the larger aspects of social existence.

Such a teacher is not made in a school of education. He can only be born there. It takes perhaps three to ten years in the classroom to make a good teacher. All the myriad overlapping interlocking courses in the catalogues of schools of education will never do it.

Schools of education are fair game for the critics of modern education. They contain some of the worst teachers and they support some of the worst teaching in the country, but proportionally no greater than is found in any of the other professional schools. We still maintain the myth of the academic excellence of the liberal arts colleges and today, with the epidemic teacher shortage there is a willingness to mass-produce teachers out of liberal arts graduates by means of hot-shot, so-called professional courses in the summer sessions of schools of education. Thus, the very people who accuse the teacher factories of doing a bad job set up situations in which they are forced to turn out an even more inferior product.

Granted that a good teacher must be a well educated person. A liberal arts graduate, just by virtue of a diploma is not such a person. He may have been subjected to more "content" than a man from a school of education and his inquiring mind may have survived that subjection. How many college graduates profess any of the intellectual curiosities they enjoyed as undergraduates? How many survive the picayune courses of inveterate scholars piling dustheaps of knowledge into the dark corners of general ignorance? What profit is there in attending the ritual of complaint of some researcher who resents the hours away from lab or library? What esthetic competence can be assured after exposure to the ruminations of some resident poet or novelist who harbors a profound distaste for freshman scribblings?

Education is a serious business and teaching is the most earnest of professions. In this business we have played the numbers racket too long and the percentages are running against us. In the teaching of specific skills, we in the United States are inferior to none. In solving social, technological and even economic problems, we are often brilliant. In the fields of scholarly competence we have lifted standards beyond the weak reach of the exhausted countries, although on occasion they do surprise us, but we are still to achieve in general education anything like the imagined excellence that has been claimed for the so-called classical education. The goal there was the development of an all-around personality capable of identifying and analyzing problems, able to be fully at home in the world, unafraid of accident, willing to accept the responsibilities of leadership, equally willing to take on the burdens of unrequited labor, a person for whom service to humanity is not a pulpit catch-phrase, and self-respect is not a badge of intellectual snobbery. This is demanding a lot of the teacher but anything less will short-change our youth and ultimately corrupt our society.

We seek stability-in-motion in this society. We wish to ride herd on change and make it serve us better than ever before. The world is various, beautiful and new. There is no certitude that lasts forever and certainty is surely death. But we are placing into our children's hands power to literally reach the stars and unless they can be taught to read with wisdom and act with occasional humility, their children may have only memories of "giants in other days." We are required then to teach the method of intelligence. To teach them how to interpret the dial and counter readings of the machines they will make to extend the power of their senses; to teach them how to select appropriate ways of doing things from among a thousand competing alternatives; to teach them how to depend upon the decisions of intelligence without excluding the creative hunch that makes "the things that never were" commonplace.

6

The Use of the Book
in Changing the World

A book can stabilize ideas. It can also pry things loose. Copernicus, in the closeness of his study, finished the writing of his great work, *De Revolutionibus* and was afraid. Archimedes, almost two thousand years before, had said that if he were given a place to stand and a long enough lever he could literally move the world. Copernicus did just this with the power of his mind and the strength of his pen. He withheld the publication of his book for thirty-six years, but even then it was greeted with laughter, derision and fear.

There are two kinds of books that change the world; one broadcasts its message to the people in philosophical, moral, poetic or political language. This is the way of the New Testament, The Koran, the Analects of Confucius, Luther's Theses, *Pilgrim's Progress,* Calvin's Institutes of the Christian Religion, the Bill of Rights, the Communist Manifesto. They are essentially calls to social action. Depending on who you are you will probably object to the juxtaposition of some of these titles. The list is merely descriptive. It is not exhaustive. You will want to revise it. You may object at first to the inclusion of the Communist Manifesto—but think. You are suffering its consequences, and consequence is the only criterion here.

The other kind of book is the one Copernicus wrote. Most people cannot read it in its time. Most of the rest will not. Its author may be burned, bludgeoned, buried alive or ignored. The social effect of the book may be sudden or slow but when its consequences are

great, they are world-shattering and world-building. These books are
usually what we loosely call scientific. They seek to describe things
as they are. They may be philosophical, and in their own idiom they
may even be poetic but they are never widely read. These books are
really modern inventions. In fact they signal the birth of modern
times. Many of them were written within the span of 150 years:
Agricola's *Concerning Metals* (1546—he is called the father of min-
eralogy), Vesalius' *On the Fabric of the Human Body* (1543—the
first great work of science, a keystone of modern biology), *De
Revolutionibus* (1543—in which the author sent the earth spinning
on its axis around the sun, no longer the stable center of a fixed
universe), Galileo's *Discourses Concerning Two New Sciences* (1638
—divorcing physics and mechanics from theology). Galileo was a
practical man who saw no reason why he should sacrifice himself
in defense of his scientific principles; if they were valid they could
defend themselves. They did. His magnum opus was *Dialogue on
the Two Chief Systems of the World* (1632), in which he contrasted
the ptolemaic and the Copernican world views, demonstrating the
inadequacy of the former. Rene Descartes, the first modern philosopher wrote his views on the nature of the universe in *The World*
(1633), withdrew the book when he heard that Galileo was having
difficulty, and instead published his great *Discourse on Method*
(1637), in which he organized and made explicit the essential methods of modern science. Newton capped this century-long assault
with his youthful monographs on mechanics. His *Principia* (1687)
summed up his life work. The modern age was born. From the
birth of Copernicus in 1473 to the death of Newton in 1727 all of
these great works and a round dozen more were the signatures of
the modern world's birth certificate. The eighteenth and nineteenth
centuries produced whole libraries of useful and important work in
the sciences and, in philosophy, there were Leibnitz, Kant and
Hegel, but the next really great world-shaping work was Darwin's
Origin of the Species in 1859. Man was now a part of the universe,
not an unwitting voyager alone and afraid "in a world he never
made."

The lists are incomplete. The two categories are inadequate. Freud turned the inner world inside out. Einstein sent the whole universe spinning in a flatter trajectory. The nuclear physicists dug deeper into the infinitesimal. The astro-physicists have reached farther into the infinite. The psychologists catalogued man's moods, motives and mechanisms. The medical scientists teamed up with the plumbers and made most of the bad bugs that bother man behave. The engineers have wound time around their fingers, shrunk the earth to a day-long ride, liberated and leashed power that was never ascribed to the gods and, with the physical scientists, made man potentially the greatest source of geologic change the world has ever known. In the sign of the mushroom cloud we read quicker death and greater dignity for the children of men. They have but to learn to choose appropriately and Eden's gate will open wide.

The men who wrote these books are the great generalizers, systematizers and simplifiers. They are never easy to read. The "simple" clear statement, such as you will find in school-book versions of Newton's laws of motion or in the enunciation of any scientific "law," requires for its understanding, a kind of reading that we are all too prone to leave to specialists. Yet we often require children to mouth these statements like ritual words of catechism.

How much understanding is represented by a boy's uttering the words, "A body at rest tends to remain at rest unless acted upon by an outside force." Ask yourself the meanings of the objects of all those prepositions. Suppose you were to demonstrate, operationally, the sum of these meanings. What other issues or problems would need further inquiry? If all things move, can there be rest? Or is rest relative to other degrees of motion? Then it would seem that bodies are always being acted upon. But from where? What *is outside* anyway? This questioning could be extended and it might even be profitable as an exercise in one kind of thinking but what needs emphasis here is that in any kind of teaching the teacher is ultimately confronted with the task of teaching someone how to read. This point is overlooked even after pious statements are made about all teachers being teachers of reading. The science teacher sometimes acts as if all that is required for the effective use of his textbook is the accession of new scientific words to the child's vocabulary. For that matter the math teacher and the social science teacher may feel the same way.

The job of reading instruction is often assumed to have been completed by the sixth grade. Those who cannot then read are, of course reading problems. It is still very difficult for most teachers to accept the notion that "reading readiness," that almost magical psychological point at which the child is ready to begin to read, is not a phenomenon peculiar to the early grades. Some children are delayed, for emotional as well as for physiological reasons, well past the tenth year in reading. Some others, very few to be sure, continue to experience difficulties into the early high school years.

We are only beginning to produce enough teachers with training adequate to the solution of these problems. The fact that we are concerned, that we strive so to give every child adequate reading abilities is again a reflection of our assumption that every child be educated. But there are a few of the more extreme cases that still persist—the boys and girls for whom reading of any sort beyond the price-tag and headline level is hardly worth the effort. They are not necessarily stupid but it is doubtful that the resources of an educational system will ever be great enough to arouse their interests in reading per se. They will continue to pick up information through the visual and auditory media. They will learn a great deal by making models and charts and doing the housekeeping chores about the room. There is much we have still to learn about educating them but the real reading problem is with the so-called good readers, who perversely do not understand what they read.

There is this easy, conscience-salving prejudice into which a teacher can fall. Our measurements of intelligence in the schools is still mainly on the verbal scales. Those who make low scores and yet appear on other evidence to be bright are labeled "non-verbal," "non-academic," "thing-oriented," etc. At any rate they are excluded from the select center of the teacher's attention. Most of them will terminate their formal education sometime during the high school career. In the majority of cases this is an appropriate decision on social, psychological and economic grounds. The sad fact is that we have not yet put into operation on a wide enough scale the kind of education which for them would be most meaningful and useful. They need to have much of the information about their world that the rest of their classmates will eventually get through reading. They get only the scraps from the feast. The amount of learning that they do with television, ill-assorted though it is, is considerable. They learn well with the film, the demonstration and the kind of work in which they actually do something. They represent a special and important problem to which we must return later in the book.

The role of the subject-matter teacher, as a teacher of reading skills, is only dimly being recognized. The science teacher, for example, recognizes well enough the special kinds of reading required in dealing with charts, graphs, formulae and instruments. He teaches this readily and well. He is inclined to blame the English teacher, the elementary school teacher and, where one exists, the reading teacher when he is faced with a reading problem in an apparently literate class. Actually he is facing a terrifically exciting challenge to teach another new aspect of reading. It is not merely a problem of extending a vocabulary. We have seen that this is a continuing process throughout all school life. He has an opportunity of formalizing a way of thinking that is probably implicit in democratic life; the habit of thinking about things that are vital in terms of what will happen if we act in a certain way. This is not merely common-sense thinking, although common sense tends to operate this way. More important, it is a tendency to weigh alternative courses of action, to do this openly in a community of others who might be affected by the outcome of any decision; to submit what is developed or discovered to public examination and finally to abide by the action decided upon.

The character of such thinking is eminently social. Thinking about the concrete facts that are found in the textbook, discovered in classroom experiment, or recognized in first-hand experience provides the student, with the teacher as guide, with an opportunity to make sound generalizations about the physical world in which he lives. In order to be able to do this the student must see relations among facts and so follow the author's or the teacher's line of reasoning. It must put him in a position to test the validity of the conclusions that are reached. This is difficult, however, with a textbook or a teacher who violates the student's intelligence by splitting the nature of things into indigestible packets.

Too many science texts make science either sheer drudgery or a denatured formality. Physics in these books is little more than a study of levers, wheels and pulleys, with a biographical addendum about men of science in the nineteenth and twentieth centuries. Electricity, optics and acoustics may be separated out for special consideration. The illustrations, especially when they are photographic, are usually outdated. Imagine what a child thinks on seeing pictures of antiquated electronic components, when he has been tinkering with transistors and printed circuits for years. But the worst feature is the formalisms. Just as it is nonsensical to begin the teaching of reading with a formal learning of the alphabet, so is it equally meaningless to introduce the pupil to abstract statements of scientific laws. We are actually asking him to do something that very few mature scientists can do without considerable effort; to start with the basic statements of the several sciences and build an articulated symbolic model of the universe.

The world, for all children and most adults is all of a piece. We do not think of water in terms of its discrete properties. We don't look at electric light in terms of incandescence, radiation and molecular vibrations. We don't listen to a sound as a wave-form. Yet even the introductory books on so-called general science begin by taking the world apart rather than taking it all of a piece. The bright and wonderful universe is shattered into dull shards.

How can children, thus abused, be introduced to the exciting history of world shaping ideas? We have referred to the great books that record the growth of science. We could have chosen any of the books that presented new ways of looking at the world. They too would be inaccessible to minds dulled by index-card textbooks. Consider for a moment some of the ideas that provide the basic structure of our society. Did they just happen? Were they "revealed" to man? Are they aspects of the nature of things? What about human dignity and the ultimate preciousness of the individual? What of social equality? How about written law as a constant for the measurement of changing values? How about values themselves? What are they? Where do they come from? What makes them change, or do they? What is the nature of human nature? Is it fixed or variable? What different ways has man's role in the universe been conceived? Were the times and societies in which these different notions had currency different from each other and from us? Was this difference a result of these different world views? What kind of social and intellectual climate is required or was required for the birth of what we know as science? What of religion and the religious experience? Can we find sources for this elsewhere than in the human psyche? Does what we say about how we know anything, affect what in fact we do know?

"What is the stars?" asks Sean O'Casey's character. The reply is, "That is philosophy." Well, what of philosophy? For most of us it is a subject withdrawn from common use, or else it is the substance of comic characters or the prose-skeleton on which the meat of a beer commercial is hung. What indeed is philosophy? Why, it bakes bread. It marks out the world and makes it manageable. It is the way we see things we could never see before. It locates sources of value. It touches the hem of the triple goddess of truth, goodness and beauty. It is man thinking up purposes and thinking towards purposes. It is the golden thread of willful wisdom man uses to escape the labyrinth of ignorance. Eventually it is wrong or inadequate or both. But right there is another source of man's thinking strength. Philosophy is the contract man makes with himself, his fellows, and the universe. It may be open for re-examination by any of the parties without prior warning, and yet even during negotiations it remains in force. It is the ultimate publisher's contract behind all the books that have or ever will have the power to change the world.

The causes of change in this world are many but the greatest cause of all is man himself. In the very act of gaining new knowledge in one direction, he confounds himself in another. The confounding is useful. It is the gateway to new experiences and eventually to new knowledge. We pick our way in the darkness with book, brain and measuring rod. The book is the atlas of possible worlds and a gazetteer for the probable ones. Books have changed the world many times. They are changing it now; sometimes for good, sometimes for ill, but far more often for man's betterment. In our books we place the tables, the charts, the logbook records of our past voyages of exploration. In our books we enter the "true courses" for new horizons and report strange landfalls made on midnight seas.

We ask the school to be both chartroom and navigational bridge but the family must share in providing some of the instruments. It must in fact be the ship itself. For unless the family is hospitable to the play of ideas, or at least not hostile, the child's wonder will shrivel into dull acceptance of things as they are and change will become the nightmare terror of tiny loneliness.

There is no simple surety against this. The mere possession of books provides no amulet. A family where ideas are entertained, for their own sake, where child curiosity is matched by adult care and interest, will, whatever its intellectual or educational limitations, at least assure its children a running start towards humane understanding and a useful life. The little child loves to be read to, and through childhood the doors of the book are always open. The adolescent is deserted in a forest of changing fears. The little child is cuddled in the warm parental lap. When the child is delivered at the door of the school, that nightly reading quickly becomes an onerous chore and is soon dispensed with entirely. Oh, Mama will "hear" him read, and scold when "mistakes" are made. Little failures bring big lumps in the throat and past delight becomes present drudgery. Reading, which seemed so easy, so accessible, so natural, becomes a fake and a fraud. Soon everyone is embarrassed by the presence of the open book. The childish treasure is consigned to the attic or given away or discarded. All that remains is the toilsome "reader" that teacher warns must be covered in wrapping paper or stronger stuff despite the fact that school books have an almost armor-plated toughness.

Of course, the teacher will rescue most of these children. And most families are nowhere nearly as bad as all this. But some are and they are the ones that contribute an overplus of "reading failures" to school and society. The rest of us are small sinners but our venial sins are terrible flaws when they come between the growing groping mind of the child and the inviting field of the book. There is a corrective. The mother who initiated her child's "reading" with the story of the beautiful day, the father whose great voice rumbled the magic of the book, must continue their own reading and learning, with ever increasing interest as the child grows up. The adolescent who is annoyed by his parents' increasing obtuseness and stupidity should at least have the comfort of knowing that this is only in the area of human relations. He needs the assurance that the strange feelings he has inside, do not make him dangerously different from the human race; that his growing uniqueness is "normal." He needs to be reassured that he is important as a human being. Younger children are positive on this score, teenagers are not. He needs, above all else, to try out, to audition for some life work. For it is frightening to discover that you are not the center of the universe. It is terrifying to feel that you are odd and queer. It is exhausting to consider the prospect of choosing from a million possible roles to play.

Reading presents the possibilities of just such dry runs, of adventures without wounds, of defeats without death and a thousand rebirths of character to be had at the price of a book and the time it takes to read it. What are such books? Where can you get them? Well, there are all sorts of lists to be had for postage or a small fee. Each has some value, but the major shortcoming of all is that they are and must be designed for specific purposes usually associated with the deliberate educative function of the schools. Any good teacher can and does make up such lists for her own use in particular classes. She constantly revises them, and, to the degree that they are effective for her, they are that much less useful to anyone else. This is not to say that parents shouldn't seek help in the purchase of books for their children. The best help is close at hand, the child itself. Take the boy or girl on regular shopping tours to bookstores and libraries, where they are accessible, and then to catalogues, where they are not. Make the acquisition of books a family enterprise. Use the book-review sections of the local papers and popular magazines. Subscribe to the *Saturday Review,* or the *New York Times* Book Review. Join some book clubs but don't allow them to high-pressure you into "cultural" purchases. Don't fall for the high-pressure advertising gimmicks such as the reading profile offered occasionally by one of the biggest of these organizations. Your problem is that of developing in yourselves and in your children the ability of making useful choices in the areas where family and individual interest are running highest. Beware of literary societies and reading clubs. They are almost always the hobby-horses of rather strange equestrians. Cultivate the friendship and the intelligence of your local librarian. She can make resources accessible to you beyond your financial means.

You may own a wall of books which you dust religiously. You may be a "reader" in the descriptive sense, but as a parent, concerned with the growth of your child's personality, you have to be an active reader, one in whom the quality of wonder hasn't died, one in whom the adventure in ideas has a positive participant. For what the book has to offer in this changing world is the stability to make change meaningful. What it offers to those who will change the world, both you and your children, is the lever of intelligence and the point of vantage from which it may be employed. Our literal time has been circumscribed by the drawn and quartered hour of radio and television. The book defeats and recreates time. It permits the quiet pause; it permits extended reflection; it is an invitation to consider and contend with the mind of the author and his creative ideas. This is not written in the accents of the pedant or the antiseptic scholar. This is not the argument-from-excellence, nor is it a plea for Culture. The broadest intellectual literacy is our goal, a literacy that goes far beyond the basic ability to know where you are and what it costs you, a literacy in which intelligence in dealing with matters of practical consequences is widely exercised and against which the cant and confusion of the soap-seller is ineffective.

As we have seen repeatedly, there are many ways of reading and many reasons for reading. We read the phone book at great speed to get a single bit of information. We read instructions and directions with diffidence and almost a touch of fear. We may read the backs of breakfast-food cartons as absently as we would watch a passing crowd. We may read our way into a novel, yearning to be possessed by the pulse and rhythm of the author's story or style, or perhaps fighting against the seduction of his ideas. But, however we read, our reading is never a simple act.

There are some aspects of reading that have always been onerous. It requires a level of muscular and mental coordination, a degree of attention, when it is purposeful, like no other human effort. This is especially true during the years when we are developing the skills it requires. Through the centuries the publishers and book manufacturers have tried to lighten this burden by improving type faces, and inks and papers, and by many other means from their vast and ever growing storehouse of knowledge and experience. But ultimately the struggle for meaning must remain between the individual reader and his book; a struggle which must be solitary and may often be glorious. This struggle has been, and in some ways it must always remain a source of much that is good and great in the individual.

Reading is a two-way process, between what someone writes, and what someone understands, and the sometimes awful difference between the two. It also involves what happens because of this understanding. The literary experience—for this kind of reading is that above all else—is one of the most profound, mind-shaping experiences in the life of man. It makes it possible for Plato and Christ to instruct us from thousands of years away. It joins minds and times together for the better management of our universe. It is as abstract as the idea of good. It is as precise and as practical as a door latch. It is the golden goad that makes man humane. It is this that we want our children to learn. For it is through the record that others leave to us in fact and fancy that we human beings live so richly in so short a time.

Part Two

Part Two

7

How Do You Read?

In many primitive tribes, boys are shown how to draw the tracks of animals in the earth and to imitate the cries of these animals. The cry becomes the name of the beast and the track becomes the sign of the sound. The boy is being taught to read.

Whenever a man or a group of men have developed a system of signs, be they broken twigs or scratches on rocks, they are confronted with the task of teaching someone to read them if the signs are to be used for anything more than private memory aids. The first writer was the first reading teacher. Throughout the vast history of Egypt, the scribe was always an important person. A father advises his son:

Set to work and become a scribe, for then thou shalt be a leader of men. The profession of scribe is a princely profession, his writing materials and his rolls of books bring pleasantness and riches.[1]

Elsewhere, in this ancient scroll called the *Teaching of Duauf,* (1300 B.C.) the father prays:

Would that I might make thee love books more than my mother, would that I might bring their beauty before thy face. It is greater than any other calling.[2]

The Egyptians had devised a system of phonetic signs and long before the fourth millennium they had reduced it to an alphabet

[1] Cited in Frederick Eby and Charles Flinn Arrowood, *The History and Philosophy of Education, Ancient and Medieval,* Englewood Cliffs, N. J.: Prentice-Hall, 1940, p. 85.
[2] *Ibid.*

of twenty-four letters. Some scholars claim that the Egyptians took their ideas from even earlier Sumerian scripts, and this may be so; but it was the Egyptians who developed the strange idea that he who writes rules the world. In the Louvre, there is a wonderfully realistic statue of an Egyptian scribe, squatting before his manuscript armed with a pen in one hand and a similar weapon in reserve behind his ear. He is one of the "rabble of low degree," the perennial clerk, dependable, meticulous and apparently uncomplaining "with just enough intelligence," as Will Durant remarks, "not to be dangerous." [3] In his meager spare time he nurses his complaints against the world and fashions them into imperishable verse of no consequence, probably trying to write the Great Egyptian Novel!

Wherever writing starts, however it begins, it marks the greatest step we ever take towards civilization. The earliest scribe was probably a combination checker and straw-boss for some stevedoring outfit on the Lower Nile. He kept lists, devised bills of lading and invented literature. The priestly writings were already older but this scribe's scribbling had to be public if there was to be any commercial profit. The Phoenician merchantmen, in their long low ships, picked up the marked goods and peddled them along the Mediterranean coasts and so got a reputation in the underdeveloped areas as the inventors of the alphabet. By Homer's time the Greeks had picked up this system of notation, calling it by its first two letters, their own pronunciation of the Semitic names Aleph and Beth. The Phoenicians were good middlemen, they were never inventors.

The scribes, whatever their position, rarely had time to teach, and probably as is the case today, they would not have made very good teachers. It was the priests who gave the basic instruction in the four R's and it was the teacher's job to produce the clerical help for the state. Then, as today, the teacher spread the propaganda that the white-collar job gives dignity, status and security, but there is

[3] Will Durant, *Our Oriental Heritage*, New York: Simon and Schuster, 1942, p. 160.

an old papyrus in which the poor teacher complains that his pupils love beer more than they like books. Things have been ever thus.

Reading which has to do with the facts of the case, whether it is a load of bricks or a bale of cotton, is restricted to "counting off" what is before us. And for this kind of reading the Egyptian teacher instructed his pupil to "Let thy mouth read the book in thy hand . . . ." This is fine for items of trade. It is almost useless for abstract ideas. The mind runs ahead of the mouth. It wants precise directions and accurate descriptions of things as they are. With this kind of information we learn how better to control things. But a book can be a shackle to thought.

When a scroll of writing is labeled sacred, what it contains must be revered, be it ink blot or idea. The scribe may stand on the river bank and struggle for accuracy in his listings but the scribe on the temple floor with the papyrus spread out before him must let his mouth read the book and apologize to the gods for the sins of his lips.

From the ancient beginnings in temple and storehouse, writing and reading follow two courses that sometimes are parallel, sometimes identical, but usually are separate. There is magic in the written word that multiplies the potency of the spoken one.

Whatever we learn we never forget, at least not entirely. This is true of the individual as well as of the society. Forms of behavior that were appropriate to the Cro-Magnon man undoubtedly persist today. We certainly have evidence in historical time of the survival of ancient attitudes, beliefs and actions. The Easter service in a New York cathedral and the springtime fertility rites in Stonehenge are first cousins. Remnants of feudalism bestrew our lawbooks and reiterate ancient injunctions. We christen an atomic submarine with a ceremony little different from that of the old Greeks. We put no stock in a dozen superstitious acts which, nonetheless, we commit every day. Many skyscrapers have no thirteenth floor and we risk vehicular death rather than walk beneath a window cleaner's ladder. Yesterday's ritual may become today's recreation, but we challenge wornout gods with caution.

So it is with reading. The priestly Egyptian scribe revered each word and respected every mark on his papyrus. The modern "party of the second part" signs on the dotted line and regards with fear, trembling and very little understanding, the awesome meaning of the black little words. The monkish scholar in the medieval monastery, crouching within the protecting circle of a guttering tallow lamp, kisses the vellum page spelling out with fearsome love the sacred phrases of an unknown prayer. A schoolboy in a glass-walled classroom recites the opening phrases of "My Country tears of free . . ." or pledges allegiance to "the flag of the United States and the revolution for which it stands . . ."

The word committed to paper somehow gathers a life of its own and verifies itself by the fact of its existence. We may laugh at the person who says "It must be true I read it in the papers." We will nod sagely when someone declares that "It is a scientific fact that . . . (something is so)." The powerful little word "is" can tie together things that have no possible connection, and make them appear to be identical. The expression, "It is written" carries with it the finality of "This is the truth." It is the seeming heritage of the so-called Dark Ages that what has been committed to writing is incontrovertible. Historically this is not so, for of all classes and degrees, the scholar is most prone to bickering and hair-splitting. Many ancient texts bear the prescript "Against Thus and So."

It is tempting to characterize the ways men read their books in different times as expressive of the life they lived. This is as easy to do as it is inaccurate. Of course Isadore of Seville, a scholarly monk, at the beginning of the seventh century, composed a great encyclopedia in which he attempted quite successfully to desecularize all knowledge. He was anti-scientific. He placed no reliance upon the value of direct observation and urged complete subservience to authority. He was not interested in his contemporary affairs or the mere business of living. From the smug hindsight of history he reflects all that was "wrong" with the early Middle Ages. But the point to be remembered is that there is no one way to read a book, and perhaps there never was. The written histories tell of the dark places of yesterday where men struggled to keep alive a spark of ancient wisdom. They tell of the primitive at the verge of history scratching magical signs on soft rock. They tell of priests forming a closed shop of information and protecting their trade secrets through a thousand years. But the very existence of these books tells another story. When massive reproduction of the written word became possible, mass access to information became unavoidable. The rabble began to read its way out of the darkness. The guardians of the word were slowly routed and civilization was shifted to a paper-and-ink standard.

Today the book is a highly efficient instrument. It is as simple or as complicated as its content. It contains only open secrets. Whatever is written down and printed is susceptible to some kind of understanding. It may not be what the author intended. He may and does often claim that he is misread. He can only defend himself by more writing. He may succeed in weaning his public away from himself but his books and his ideas will have a life of their own.

The history of man's reading can be divided into three major areas; a primitive period in which he made and learned the letters of an alphabet and spelled them out, reading word by word. Next there were the dark ages when some kind of production line techniques were established through the employment of copyists whose accuracy and output were highly variable functions. Here books, regardless of their contents were greatly respected and the word on the page was revered. Scholars marshaled their forces behind the books to prevent the vulgar masses from knowing the trade secrets of wisdom. Authority and authorship were synonymous. Knowledge was not gained, it was given. Thinking was divorced from the test of action. It is with Gutenberg's creaking press that we enter the age of man, in which the book almost immediately becomes a high speed intellectual power tool.

When everyone may read, no man need be vulgar and the storehouses of our heritage are broached for the benefit of all. The loudest sound man has ever made is the banging of a frame of type on the bed of a printing press. It has continued to echo around the world, sounding democratic themes in the minds of men. This may appear to be a large and even an unwarranted claim, for evil things have come from books, too. Yet it is the nature of the public book that anyone can eventually get to it, examine it, test its claims in the open market place of ideas. Freedom at all levels of inquiry and in all aspects of human discourse is a consequence of the available book. Freedom is the label we put on all the things and acts that can be managed and controlled. Control is the doing of things purposively, with awareness of what is wanted. Freedom is not an abstract concept like beauty, nor is it free-swinging, undirected license. Freedom is what most directly characterizes the open society. It includes authority, not as Isadore of Seville understood that term but rather as the expression of the relationships among the regularities and changes that occur in the world. Freedom embraces responsibility, not as mere obedience to prescribed or contractual activities, but as the willingness to entertain and to accept the consequences of our own acts and those of which we approve. Freedom is the driver's license man has for the operation of everything from parliaments to can openers. He revokes it whenever he destroys the neat balance that must be maintained among thought, feeling and act. This balance can be kept only by a careful and continuous shifting of weights and values among these three. It requires a careful and constant reading of the world and its reflection on the faces of people and books.

The books that have changed the world and those that are changing it now, the books that keep it steady enough for us to see it whole, the books that are the time machines that take us back to the birth of dreams and disasters and all our early triumphs; they are all magical instruments for defense, instruction and delight. When everyman may learn to live the lives of the seekers and sufferers, the dreamers, lovers and losers of everytime, then he is able to reach beyond his father's grasp to freedom. For the book is, ✓ finally, the great immortalizing machine. It can take what happens once and make it live forever and no man's hopes or fears or mistakes need ever be forgotten.

The teachers in our schools know this. It is implicit in their work. It is bedded deep in those unarticulated major assumptions they share with all of us about the kind of world we want to live in. Most of them would be hard pressed to make it explicit, many would be impatient with the task. Philosophical discourse is often a tedious affair. But look to the classrooms and watch them at work. As you have taught your child to use your language, they are teaching him to read its signs.

The basic elements in the teaching of reading skills are similar to those needed and gained in the spoken language. But the attention given to early language instruction is not all matched in reading. Of course we read to the child and in some instances even lavish it with gifts of beautifully colored books. A great deal of this is simple and quite legitimate selfishness, for there is much personal pleasure to be derived from introducing the child to the magical stories of our own childhood. But we give it nothing like the attention we expend upon the spoken word, mainly because the returns are so small. Whereas the child gains quickly in a basic spoken vocabulary, it will be years before it begins to be concerned with specific words in a book. In this instance it is all outlay on the part of the parent. It is a large investment in time and energy, but it is a safe investment too, if we could only realize it. The loving care that we extend to the child in the years before school life begins can pay handsome dividends in its psychological and social security. For with the exception of those very few children who suffer terrible psychological injuries which may be reflected in a reluctance to engage in reading, the boy or girl to whom both parents and other family members give the kindness and courtesy of more than just the ritual bedtime book, will enter the adventure of self-reading in a happy, welcoming frame of mind. But too often parents use the book as a bedtime bribe, as a device by which the child can be trapped into sleep, a sleep which releases the parents from further exhausting social intercourse with the child.

This is no plea for the bookish family. There are too many other ways in which we get our entertainment and instruction for us to depend upon any single source, but the book has virtues that are shared by no other medium of communication. It has become more valuable as its uses become less general. The modern child is introduced to the wonders of television even before he makes the acquaintance of the book and in some homes he will hear the sound of the radio as early as he can distinguish his mother's voice. But the book is still the master of "quietness and slow time." It does not quarter the hour to the huckster's rant. It sells nothing but ideas and feelings, remembrances and hopes. The reader alone controls the pace. The book will wait a minute, a year, a lifetime. It will say again, tirelessly, what it has said well once. And in a family where books are used, where they are at once the "furniture of the home and the furnishings of the mind" both quietness and excitement will be equally accessible and the rhythm of living need not be geared to the pulse of the commercial's chant.

In such a home book reading will be introduced to the child. It will never be a bribe but a shared adventure. It will be a symbol of enjoyment, a sign of living curiosity, a signal for the inquiring mind. In such a home the parents will read with the child, sharing the twice-told pleasures. And finally, the child's entrance into school will not be a painful rite-of-passage but an extension of the horizons already anticipated.

Most of us have forgotten or only vaguely remember our own school experiences in reading. Most of them were undoubtedly as pleasant as they still are for today's child. We were occasionally bored by the necessarily deliberate regimen of the classroom. A teacher of thirty children cannot be as profligate with time as the mother of one or two. The classroom library, where it exists at all, cannot always be as rich as the child's own bookshelf. But the quality of the reading experience at school is a vastly different one which has to be seen in considerable detail if it is to be fully appreciated and understood.

Although experiments in the teaching of reading have been going on for more than half a century now, there is general agreement among the psychologically informed on these points: the development of reading skills is a continuous process in which certain specific stages can be seen. For convenience here seven specific periods will be described. They are not to be considered as discreet, in fact the first stage persists in some form throughout all the others. Some will care to question the number and the arbitrariness of the distinctions. They are offered mainly for ease of description and where possible the interrelations will be indicated.

The first stage is appropriately called the reading-readiness period. For most children this usually occurs at the beginning of the first grade. Many children can be taught to read much earlier but most teachers still feel that it is not the teacher's role to make performing seals or monstrously successful Quiz Kids. Her job is to perceive and to pace the child's growth. This initial reading-readiness period is not the last one of its kind but it can be the most important. If the child is pushed too suddenly, or too far, or if the readiness is not soon enough responded to, all kinds of difficulties may arise which may take a long time to overcome.

During the reading-readiness period the child, with the teacher's guidance, develops ways of getting information, general skill in eye movement and the control of interest, all of which are necessary if he is to read with success. But no child comes to this experience empty-handed. He has years of successful language experiences behind him. He has become adept in communicating his wants and his feeling and has considerable skill in understanding the needs and desires of others. He has learned to adjust his language to the person or group he happens to be with, but all of this learning has been closely tied in to the practical business of living. At the very beginning of his school reading experience he must also have practical needs for reading if the whole affair is not to become a miserable chore. He must "get something" from reading just as he "gets something" from talking and listening. His readiness to read is indicated by his expressed desire to get this something.

If we return for a moment to the broad idea of reading that was

offered in the first chapter we can see that from the very beginning
all of the child's school experiences are directed toward increasing
his skill in "reading his world." The kindergarten is a wonderful
place where things are the right size for children. Here there are all
kinds of exciting pictures at the child's eye-level. With the exception of the teacher, everyone is about the same size. It is all very
comfortable. There is a lot of time to talk. There are plenty of things
to do. It is a society of little equals. The chairs can be moved into
a circle or bunched together in little groups and the stories, there
are grand and wonderful stories that you can tell each other—and
you all *listen*. How many times, out of sheer necessity, do we defend
our egos by not listening to a child? So many questions, so very
many questions, and answers only open the sluice gates of curiosity
still wider! So we don't listen, and a child is hurt. Not a deep wound,
of course, and the scar will never be seen and in the main it con-
tributes to the tough scar tissue of useful indifference. He needs a
thick hide to withstand the friction of rubbing against other personalities. But the school is a child's world, really free from adults.
Teachers are a third species, part adult, part child, who can talk
to and for both child and adult.

School life begins where most children are most successful, with
talk. The delightful ritual of "show-and-tell" where adventures are
shared. The story hour, when the big book is opened and the teacher
dissolves the world of here and now and brings yesterwhere to the
children's feet. Game time when tribal rules are set and we can
become anything we want to be, when noise is good and no one
scolds. And the grand fights, the pushings and shovings where *I* and
mine is separated from *you* and *yours* and all are joined together
in the strong warmth of *ours*. And all the time the talk and the
listening that is mixed in with it.

All this is in preparation for the next great language experience
of the child. For the little one who enters school with poor or inadequate experience in the spoken word, who comes from a rather
barren background of experience with people and things, has to be
prepared gently for the great step forward toward the meaningful

interpretation of the language that is written down. Of course he may quickly learn to "call out" the words he sees, but reading comes only to those who can recognize and respond to *meanings*. It cannot ever be repeated too often, that what we give to the child in terms of happy and successful language experiences in the home, he will be able to incorporate into wider and more useful experiences in school and in later life. This is why such emphasis is placed upon getting the child ready to read.

It is a rather easy matter to measure the physical and the mental factors that go to make reading readiness. It is the emotional and the social factors that are often neglected. They cannot be so readily measured and charted. Yet they are closely intertwined with the learner's personality development that we neglect them to his peril. The child who fails to learn to read because he is emotionally unprepared to read and the child who has failed once in trying to read are both tied into knots and subsequent efforts can result in further difficulties.

This is why introduction to actual reading is begun so gently; a simple picture and a whole word of two or three letters, both well known to the child, both well within his daily spoken vocabulary. Word and picture are handled and talked about. The teacher writes the word, usually printing in large block letters and games are played with them. This process goes on until the child acquires about seventy-five words in a so-called sight vocabulary. Some words he can only see in terms of action, these are verb-forms; some are even more abstract showing relations such as *on, in, to, for,* etc. With even so few words, however, he is ready to move on to larger words and word groups. Right here is where the mechanical-minded begin to argue. They begin by talking about the admittedly wise necessity of using material which shows each letter in only one phonetic value such as the *g* in *get, got* and *gum,* but not in *gem* and, further, that there should be no silent letters as in *knit, gnat,* etc. But it is neither logically nor psychologically sound to jump from this to an immediate demand for basic mechanical analysis. Analysis of a kind comes quickly enough. The child can see the need of it, but as Gray says in his very useful book, *On Their Own in Reading,*

> Skill in phonetic analysis is essential for independence in identifying new printed words, but this skill should be based on fundamental understanding of how sounds and their letter symbols function in our language; and these understandings should develop as generalizations based on the child's experience with words—words which he learns visually as meaningful wholes rather than mechanically as a series of letter sounds.[4]

Gray points out that in a well-balanced reading program the child will learn a basic stock of sight words which he will learn as wholes and will also develop the skills that are necessary in getting at the meanings of new words. These skills will include the use of context clues as well as word-form clues. He will also employ phonetic word analysis and the analysis of word structure in terms of root words, prefixes, suffixes, inflectional endings and syllables, but all in good and proper time and always in meaningful reading situations —never as the kind of rote learning that old Condillac deplored.

Throughout all the stages in the development of reading skills there is a large element of play, but nowhere is it as important as in this first period. All the skill, resourcefulness and artistry of the teacher is brought to bear in devising and providing situations in which the shape, sound and use of the word can be presented. She may use rhyming games and wall charts, she may use colored charts and cards, film slides and strips, songs and chants. The children may trace out the words and some may even begin a simple kind of letter writing. The alphabet as such will be wisely held off for a while, although its immediate use is nowhere near as dangerous as some extremists think.

The "readying" period may for many children last only a few weeks and these children will begin to move on to the next stage which is really the beginning of reading as such. Here the child gets specific instruction in recognizing words with which he has

[4] William S. Gray, *On Their Own in Reading,* Chicago, Ill.: Scott, Foresman, 1948, p. 32.

already become familiar. Most children will be able to read these words smoothly and fluently and with all of the understanding that is necessary for their meanings. This is the great practice time in which the child reads from a pre-primer (a horrible word!).

The publishers have generally done an excellent job with these books, especially in format and usually in illustration too. But they occasionally assault the child's intelligence with a story and idea content that would bore a five-year-old. The books abound in sentences like "See Jack jump." "Jack get the ball." "Oh, Jack, see the ball." "The ball is red." "The red ball is in Jack's hand." First graders, however, are remarkably tolerant. They will make fun of their reading books, but they won't reject them yet.

Most of the children are now ready to move on to the next stage in which initial independent reading is begun. This might be between two and three months after the acquisition of a sight vocabulary. He will now begin to read simple connected material of several sentences in length. The teacher will be most concerned that he develop and maintain appropriate left-to-right eye movements and be able to extract full understanding from what he reads. Do we ever stop to think how important this skill is and that it has to be *taught?* Most important for all the rest of his reading growth, he will begin to acquire some of the elementary techniques for getting at the meaning of unfamiliar words. He will learn some of the basic sound values of some letter combinations, will be taught to see smaller words in the big new ones and perhaps even make a start in getting the meaning of a new word from the words around it, in other words, to use context clues. For those parents who have been frightened by the recent best-selling, but hardly best-informing, tempest, it might be comforting to note that the so-called phonic analysis is taught to the child usually within three months after the first grade has been started. And it is constantly re-emphasized. Yet phonic analysis alone is as useless, as any good analytic tool must be, until it is put to work as an adjunct to real thinking, to get at meanings.

The child reaches the next stage, sometimes called the "advanced primary reading period," about five or six months after the beginning of actual reading instruction. His sight vocabulary is now much larger. He is able to work out many context clues. His word-attack skills, as the reading teacher calls them, now include ability to use context clues, ability to work out pronunciation of words from visual, sound and phonetic elements. For the child has, as we noted in an earlier chapter, a relatively large speaking vocabulary; therefore, once he can properly pronounce a word, he can usually get at its common meaning. (It will be several years before he will begin to meet and master words he has never heard before.) The child at this stage is still a word-by-word reader who, because of this, will continue to make a number of errors in word recognition and will often fail to get the full meaning of what he reads. He will read "saw" for "was" and skip many vital little words. It is at this point that some parents begin to get anxious. They want to help, and some of their reasons for wanting to help are not very healthy.

It is not uncommon in some suburban areas and in other small closely knit communities for the use of the telephone to rise precipitously on the day the report cards are sent home. Mrs. A wants Mrs. B to know how well little Miss A is doing, but only after making quite sure that little Master B is floundering. It is a nasty business, with the child being goaded into a ratrace. No matter how careful the school may be in instructing the parents that no two children can or should be expected to proceed at the same rate, some parents are more concerned with their child's doing better than a neighbor's than in his learning securely to do as well as he can.

Most reading problems begin as parent problems. The best advice here is to work closely with the school, be instructed by it, help only when and in the manner it suggests. Give the child a sense of continuing achievement. He deserves it because he is making it. If you want to hear the child read, please be a respectful audience. Above all, continue your own reading habits and make them better and more consistent. Continue to read to the child, *but don't use his school books for reading material.* Be patient, be gentle, be generous with praise.

By the middle of the second grade most of the children enter a transition period from primary to intermediate reading. The main concern of the teacher here is to help the child move from the word-by-word reading to reading "thought units" that more closely approximate the rhythmic pattern of the spoken language. Emphasis is continued on development of word-attack skills and ability to handle polysyllabic words is increased. *Word perception* is here refined to the point where the child can recognize phrases or word combinations at a glance and a beginning is made in reading word groupings. It is this ability that will eventually make him an efficient reader. This transition period is a rather long one in most instances, lasting into the third grade and even very much later in some cases. The books here continue to be interesting for the child though even now he may begin to be critical, and rightly so of some of the content. He begins to read for many reasons, to find out things, to get a story, to learn the words of a song.

The intermediate reading stage is a great plateau which extends beyond the sixth grade and in some cases well into junior high school. During this period the child can now give himself more fully to thought. He is more and more on his own in his reading. He can and does begin to be critical of what he reads. He learns to evaluate the written word in terms of what it claims. He begins to be flexible in how he reads. A poem is to be read slowly, sometimes, some stories more rapidly and the factual material in which he has great interest he can read at speeds great enough to insure fuller understanding. For now he can read to get the main idea in a paragraph. He can search through a page or even a chapter for specific information. He is reading for *use* as well as for delight. However, the teacher does not neglect word-by-word analysis or any of the earlier skills, although the child can now be depended upon to increase these skills more and more on his own initiative. He has learned to handle the dictionary. He has acquired such rules as we have in English spelling, though of course he will forget or abuse them in strange ways.

Throughout the intermediate period the greatest and perhaps most important development is in the word-perception skills. This word perception takes place against the meaning background we have for the word. This meaning background is provided by our total experience with the word. This may be as direct as the *sting* of a bee or indirect, second-hand and vicarious, as "The stove is hot!" "The match will burn you!" The direct experience is what the teacher and parents depend on mainly for early vocabulary meaning growth. We often undervalue the other kinds of experience although we are quick to recognize its vital importance once it is brought to our attention.

Because of our vicarious experiences we stay alive. A first-hand experience with a live wire can be our last. The kinds of experiences that guarantee death or injury can make other kinds of learning useless. In general it is the sum of our experiences with the word that gives us the first clue to how someone might be using it in a new way. So it is with the children near the end of the intermediate period. By now reading has become for them a continuous operation within which four major functions can be seen; word perception, comprehension, reaction and integration.

As Gray points out,

Word perception involves two closely related phases. First, we must be able to identify the printed symbol; we must know . . . that the word . . . is *band* and not *bank*. Second, we must be able to call up or identify the meaning the author had in mind when he wrote the word.[5]

The printed word, in fact, sets off a chain reaction in which both phases are present and we move on to tackle the sum of the meanings of the words read so as to comprehend the ideas the writer wishes to communicate.

There are a great number of things that happen here. On this aspect of reading alone, Ivor A. Richards devotes a whole book, *How*

[5] *Ibid*. p. 35.

to Read a Page. He suggests in his preface that it might better be called "How to reap a page." He says:

A list of the vices of reading should put first, as worst and most disabling, the expectation that everything should be easily understood. Things worth thought and reflection cannot be taken in at a glance. The writer should, of course, have done his utmost to make things easy for us. He could have nothing (could he?) more important than *that* to do. But where there is still some difficulty remaining, let us beware of blaming it on the author rather than our own imperfect command of the language. To blame the writer will teach us nothing. To wonder if we are reading right may.[6]

This is the most difficult, and in some ways the most important aspect of the reading process; to get, as clearly as we can, an understanding of the precise meaning the author wanted us to have. He does this not only with the words he uses, but by the way he uses them and the particular combinations of words he chooses. It is reflected in the tone of his language, his style of expression and whatever feeling he can communicate to us through his words.

It is only then that we are in a position to go on to that other aspect of reading, to be able to *react* to these ideas, to think along with or against the author, to appreciate or to reject what he has to say. Finally, having achieved this in our reading, the total reading experience can then be built into the ways in which we think. We can integrate his ideas with our own. Our meaning background is further developed. We have added a little bit to our never-ending education.

This digression brings us to the final stage. Appropriately, it is called the "mature reading stage." It begins somewhere above the sixth year level in school. The vocabulary is greatly extended, skills in word recognition are equal to almost any task set them, reading is now completely silent and almost never word-by-word; in consequence, reading speed begins to climb beyond a page a minute. It can be deliberately varied according to the material and the purpose for which it is read. When this stage is reached, the child is in pos-

[6] Ivor A. Richards, *How to Read a Page,* New York: W. W. Norton, 1942, p. 12.

session of his finest tool for learning. Everything that has ever happened, every idea that has ever been conceived, all the rich experiences of the human race are open to him—if the rest of his home and school experiences have made him want to get them.

What has been described here is the reading life of a successful reader. Not every child will have such a life, nor will any one child move through these stages at a rate precisely like any other child. From the very first day, differences will be seen. For some children the readiness period may be delayed even into the second or third grade—such children have other kinds of trouble. The schools have carefully designed testing programs to estimate the levels of reading achievement and they have the resources to discover some of the causes of slowness, of retardation. They cannot alone get at some of the deep-seated problems of a social and psychological nature which impede some children. The vast majority of the children, however, are brought safely through the different stages of reading at rates of progress commensurate with their own total social, psychological and physiological development.

What has been described here is not a method of teaching reading but rather the essential sequence of learning that does take place. The fact that some people never complete this sequence is not necessarily a reflection of the inadequacies of teaching, although this is sometimes the case. Most usually it is an index of the almost universal scope of our educational enterprise. We wish to give everybody the opportunity to learn as much as possible. Not everyone is capable of as full an achievement as we might wish. But our democratic vistas must be vast!

There is no one best way for the teaching or the learning of anything. Reading is no exception. That there are some poor methods is not denied. There is a lunatic fringe to any enterprise. There are antique procedures that are preserved through lethargy, indifference and ignorance. Some are the result of a fantastic misreading of the findings of modern psychology; some result from holding blindly to traditional ways, merely because they have always been thus; some reflect an over-eagerness to experiment without first meeting the rigorous tests of scientific practicality. Whatever the cause, children suffer. They suffer needlessly when parents eschew their own continuing responsibilities and consider that they have done their duty when either or both parents attend a few P.T.A. meetings or make the yearly visit on Open School Day.

The school needs the active, persistent support and cooperation of all parents, not just the articulate minority. It needs criticism, both destructive and creative, if it is to meet the expanding needs of our society. Most of the criticism of the schools is and always has been responsible. This is why instances of the irresponsible kind are so glaring. The schools are not separate from the community, they can never be so and survive. But they can only be as good as the quality of the challenges to them are vital and sincere. Parents and teachers must ask the solemn question; "What kind of a society do we want for ourselves and our children?" and then have the courage, the intelligence and the willingness to put into operation the kinds of programs that will make that society come to pass. This is slow work. It can be thrilling. It is ultimately fruitful.

8

Reading in the Light of
Man-Made Moons

EDUCATION IS EVERYBODY'S BUSINESS! This declaration confronts the public on car-cards, billboards and television screens. The President of the United States urges citizens to act through their Parent-Teacher Association to improve the quality of the schools. Anyone's pronouncement on any aspect of education will sooner or later find its way into print. But through the welter of publicity and propaganda can be heard the old warning: "What is everybody's business is nobody's business." Reaction to an issue is not action on the problem.

Do school budgets need to be "beefed up"? Can the quality of teaching be improved? Are our children getting the kind of education they must have if they are to live successfully in this world? Should the Federal government help the local school board in any way? Can the social problems of the school be solved through legislative fiat? What can parents do to help at home? There is "mileage" in every one of these questions as a quick reading of today's newspapers and magazines will show.

Until the morning after October 4, 1957, when the first Sputnik beeped across our private heavens, only professional complainers dared to compare American education unfavorably with that of other countries. The Russians had achieved a scientific "first," apparently without benefit of theft or treason. Q.E.D., the Soviets must be doing a better job of training scientists than we have been doing. A Pandora's box of complaints was kicked open, the bins of our dirty educational linen were exposed to public view. The family feuds of schoolmen and school marms were broadcast for the dubious benefit of the astonished and embarrassed neighbors. The glacial slowness of institutional reconstruction became a torrent of agonized reappraisal—something has got to be done!

American education is a wonderful human adventure. Nothing quite like it has ever been dared by any other people. Yet we take it too easily for granted. We are too quick to lambaste it for its shortcomings especially when we are not too sure about what it is trying to do. None of us would presume to tell a doctor how to diagnose and few of us would be brash enough to try to instruct a lawyer how to manage our affairs. We may entertain such notions and even talk about them among ourselves, but in the presence of professionals we are respectfully silent. But teaching is another matter. Anyone who becomes a parent automatically becomes a critic of education. This is because of a natural desire that the child have the best of what is possible in this world. This is because the school, in the American sense, is what happens to everybody. Everyone has experience with teachers and with teaching. We think we know what it is all about.

Let us look at American education and what it dares to do. First, it is based upon the clear democratic notion that all children, whatever their backgrounds, whatever their physical and intellectual limitations, be helped to become the very best kinds of persons. By *best* is meant that they achieve the skills and the knowledge that will help them to realize as much as possible of their grandest dreams. This concept of American education is not one of leveling down all people to a kind of social least common denominator. It is the giving to everyone of the will and the desire to reach beyond his grasp.

This is the American Way. In the Soviet Union the child can be and is drafted into the service of holy science by the will of the State. We welcome the child's choice of any trade or profession. What his private enterprise dictates is more important than what any government desires. All that we dare to do is to provide an atmosphere of interest and adventure, the traditional Call of the wild frontier, and gamble on his democratic inclination to do something of value.

Yet, most of us have very modest ambitions for ourselves. But as parents, we dream great dreams. For, in our country, it is no myth that the road between the log cabin and the White House is open to all. It is a very rough road and few people in any generation go the distance, but there are worthwhile goals all along the way. Someone can be satisfied and proud to reach any one of them. So, in our schools we prepare our children to become mechanics and homemakers, beauticians and artists, salesmen and scholars, scientists and sailors. And along with this preparation we try to help them to become good citizens and eventually wise parents. We try to give to each individual what he most needs. We try to help him to discover what he can do best. But the school's biggest job is to give to every child the basic skills that each must have for any other success. Traditionally we have called these the three R's. There are fancier names for them, but whatever else they are called, the need for them does not diminish.

The so-called Reading Revolution that began with the invention of the printing press was actually the starting point of all of the other good revolutions by which modern man has made his world a happier and healthier place to live in. By making ideas and hopes and feelings of any man available to every man, the freedoms and the powers that we now take so for granted were planted in the minds of ordinary men and women. The idea of popular education itself was carried like a health-giving germ on the ink pads of the first printing presses. For a long time thereafter teaching and learning—schooling—meant only instruction in reading. But with the great educational innovators of the eighteenth and nineteenth centuries, attention was turned again to the child and to the problems of growing up happy and secure in a relatively friendly world. This was a wonderful change. Today, the effective teacher is as much concerned with her child's happiness as with his intellectual growth. But this concern, which is really the driving force of our democracy, carries a great danger. If a balance is not kept, if our love for children outweighs our responsibility to teach them how to think, they will be denied the ability to judge what is good and useful. If they cannot judge, they cannot grow up.

This kind of growing up, this maturing, is not a problem for the school alone. In fact, the school cannot even begin to solve it. It is first and foremost the family's responsibility. It is more difficult for the modern family than it has ever been before. The present generation of young parents, those whose children are between the ages of four and fourteen, are beset by more anxieties than any similar group in the past fifty years. Young enough to remember their own school experiences, they want their children to make better use of theirs. Sensitive to the changes in society, even when they cannot put their fingers on what has changed, they want to help their children to cope with a dangerously new world. Today's parents are more conscious of being parents than those who lived in the gentler age of steam and gas lighting. They get advice from a terrifying host of professionals, some of whom did not even exist when the Charleston was the teenage rage.

There are a dozen different kinds of psychologist, all ready and able to instruct, describe direct and improve all that parents should do and be. Schools are alive with specialists to do what a single teacher once tried to accomplish. Insurance companies hire experts to write expensively printed pamphlets telling mothers and fathers what to know and what to expect from their children. Newspaper columns are the sites for oracles who interpret dreams and itches to adolescent and adult alike, with never a thought to the consequences of misapplied wisdom. Lectures to the laity can be had at the flick of a TV dial on every conceivable aspect of human behavior. With such easily accessible wisdom, with such copious intellectual philanthropy, we should be on the verge of a golden age in human relations.

But our streets are infested with juvenile delinquents. Schools are called "blackboard jungles." The precious words "youth house" are used to label jails for children. A modern mutation of St. Vitus' Dance seems to have infected the minds and bodies of our youth. The family lives in embattled truce. Its members seem to have learned only enough to distrust each other.

This is an explosive situation. Newspapers, magazines and book publishers turn out torrents of advice, recriminations and warnings. Radio and TV panelists talk somberly about the low estate of educational affairs. Government officials and legislators view with alarm and sound the clarion for investigation, reorganization and implementation. The law is made tougher, and the teenager, especially, is depicted as an ill-begotten monster, born in the dark of the moon on the wrong side of the tracks. In all this clamor, the child, the family and the classroom teacher become either faceless statistics or are lost sight of entirely.

In spite of the stutter of Sputniks and the undulating wail of the Explorers, which have been translated into demands for more scientists, engineers and dial twisters, what has really been highlighted is the deep need to make the American educational dream a reality. The painful problems of integration bespeak a nationwide urge to make it so. The unorganized efforts to give teachers an adequate wage are related to it. Even the current hysteria over the actual and imagined problems of juvenile delinquency are aspects of this need. This need can be met and understood and satisfied within the actual homes of real people.

For these things have always been true of any family; where children are paid attention and respect, then love can be a motive force for happiness; where ideas are entertained joyously, no matter how strange they may be, then the child's curiosity will never die; where adult interest and child interest do not exclude each other, wonder will never perish. Where the home is the center, but never the whole of the world, the family will grow rich and healthy in the goods of fellowship and loyalties. But all this can only come to pass where the members of the family never lose the skill of talking to and listening to each other. They will come to pass when the youngest child is never excluded and where even the angriest child is never barred. If such an atmosphere is to exist, the parents themselves must begin by surrounding the child with loving, living language. Talk and song are not enough, though they are necessary. There must be the quiet communion that only the book can offer.

There is magic in the book, but it is like the magic of a safety match. It works only when it strikes the rough surface of interest. But even interest is not a self-starting mechanism. It must be nourished by far-sighted adults who prepare the child to be happy and successful in school.

There are three things that all parents should do when they send their children to school; make reading important, give the child good study and work habits, and learn how the child learns. Each of these factors is so closely related to the other two that success in one is dependent on success in the others. And while it is obvious that this is essentially the school's job, the parents must back it up with effective support.

Reading is so important that the school makes it the primary goal for all children. Everything else that the school will be able to do for the child will depend upon how well the child reads and what his attitude toward reading is. This is true in everything from finger painting to sports. This is as true for social adjustments as it is for social studies. For whatever else the school tries to do for the child, unless he becomes a literate person, he is doomed to live an inadequate life.

By its attitude then, the school declares that reading is important. But if the parents never read anything more than newspaper headlines, picture magazines and television programs, the child will discover by their actions that for them reading is of little consequence. They will undo almost everything the school tries to do.

The appalling fact that most Americans do not read has been verified time and again. Most people who do not read are ready to acknowledge it, apologize for the lack and explain it away with lame excuses. They pay lip-service to the school's program that is designed to give the children greater skills in reading.

It is not enough. Children learn not only by doing things but by seeing things done. Talk about the virtues and value of the book is never as effective as regular demonstrations by the parents of the book's worth to them. This can be done by having books in the home, books that are owned and treasured and *used* by both father and mother. Both parents should read habitually, or at the very least, and this is not dishonest, they should go through the motions of reading in the presence of the children.

This practice can never be started too early. In fact, there is so much practical information that parents need about the care and feeding of children, that they can be fully occupied for months prior to the birth of the first child. The point to be remembered here is that the business of reading must be regularized. Even for parents-to-be, for whom all reading is an apparently unrewarding chore, this is an investment that can pay rich dividends. They may even be able to break their own non-reading habit.

Very few parents need to be persuaded that they should read to children. They will buy picture books and story books and get many more from doting relatives. The snuggling, pajama-clad child being read to is a tradition that few parents would forgo, but even this palls after a while and the TV baby-sitter is focused on the tyke. And when the school doors finally admit the youngster, a sigh of relief is breathed. Now the teacher can do the reading.

But the teacher cannot do the same kind of reading. Her relation to the child is different from the parent's. Such a transfer of responsibility has a very unhappy effect upon the child. Reading becomes work from which Mama and Daddy have finally been relieved. This is how the child learns the first hurtful lesson that work is not really pleasant, that it is something other people are paid to do, that it is something you ought to avoid if you can.

Parents must be persuaded that their responsibility in such a matter as reading, as in the whole pattern of their child's education, is increased rather than diminished when the child enters school. This will seem to be contrary to the apparent professional judgment of teachers. For most of them do say that they, and only they should have charge of the teaching of the child. But this is only technically correct. Their success will depend primarily upon the material they have to work with, and upon the attitudes the child brings to the classroom.

The worst poverty a child can suffer from is the poverty of ideas. Intellectual malnutrition can produce an anemia of ideas that the best schooling in the world cannot compensate for.

This is not a warning that all must act as eggheads, but, rather, that no one can afford to despise the adventure in ideas. Ideas about right and wrong, beauty, truth and loyalty need to be experienced in real situations among actual people. They must be home-grown and specific. Here is a proposal for a kind of preventative medicine that can insure the intellectual health and vigor of the child.

1. Have books in the home, your books, adult books. Use them. Talk about them.
2. Have children's books in the home, a lot of them. Read to the child, at least through the sixth grade. Help him to learn to talk about his reading.
3. Learn what interests the child and help him to learn how to select his own books, books to stretch his mind and his imagination. Let him make choices so that he can really own the books.
4. Learn yourself what good work and study habits are, and help the child to acquire them.
5. Learn how to be interested in what the child is interested in. Do not be afraid to have ideas and opinions on these matters and share them. Learn how to listen to the child with eager patience. Give his questionings the importance they deserve.
6. Whatever your own main interest, keep abreast of science and what it is doing to this world.

The list could be made much longer and more specific, but this is a do-it-yourself job. Any adult can take it from here.

Teachers and parents and librarians too, are always eager for a new book list. The list can be a good tool, but like all tools, it can be dangerous. Especially where reading is concerned, any book seems to become the *right* book just because it is on an authoritative list. To choose the right book for the right child at the right time is a very complicated kind of choosing. Anyone who is interested in children can do it but it requires more than reading and buying. The following list is NOT the one you want. It is a sample. In order to choose the proper book you have to know just what your particular child needs, what the interests are, what stage of growing-up the child is in, whether or not the time has come to have him stretch for bigger things.

Before looking over the book list, here are some books and pamphlets which describe how children grow and learn:

The books of Dr. Gesell are standard and dependable, especially *The Child from Five to Ten*. Jean Piaget's little classic, *Language and Thought of the Child,* is available in a Meridian Books paperback. It is moderately difficult but very valuable. *These Are Your Children,* by Jenkins, Schachter and Bower, published by Scott, Foresman, is also useful. The Association for Childhood Education has many useful pamphlets. *About Children: How They Learn, Feel and Grow* is one of their best. William H. Armstrong's book, *Study Is Hard Work* (Harper and Brothers), although designed for college freshmen, outlines the major principles which must be applied to study at any age level. It is worth having.

With such information as these books provide and the attitudes that have been suggested here, young parents can wisely take the full responsibility that is necessary when they send children to school.

Education is everybody's business but no one has a greater stake in it than the young parent. It is important to work with the P.T.A. and other groups concerned with the welfare of the child in the school. It is important to help the school superintendent and his staff develop the kind of program and facilities they can prove that they must have. But above all else, parents must never relinquish their private responsibility for the day-to-day education of their own children. The goal is not more education in better and bigger schools. The goal of all American education is the development of happy, healthy and intelligent young people who can make this world a little better than it now is.

9

Why Do We Read?

At the beginning of this book reading was defined in a very broad way as the drinking in of all experience, making that experience a part of our growing, thinking, feeling selves. Later we saw that man created some wonderful tools and some truly marvelous ways of making experiences more manageable. The camp-fire storyteller, the garrulous elder who earned his aging keep with ancient bits of worked out wisdom; the strange one who, with chant and song, made heroes out of hunters and peopled the darkness with ogres and monsters and bodiless powers; the puzzler who discovered that questions somehow put things in the kind of order that made them easy to understand. All of these men were kindred and sometimes these characteristics could be found in one man. The thinker became different from the doer and this division of labor made partnership possible. Both doer and thinker shared an interest in knowing what things were and how they happened, but the "why" question was the preserve of the thinking man; in a large measure it still is.

Someone has to be spared the activities of everyday life in order to be able to stand aside and see how the whole thing looks; to see where we are and if possible, where we are going. We probably couldn't discover even with a time machine, when man first decided that he could afford this luxury, or when he converted the luxury, as he always does, into a vital necessity. But he did it. Man grubstaked his guardian-of-ideas perhaps in paleolithic times and was promptly frightened for his pains. But the fright was very different from what he felt when the giant carnivores were at his heels; he didn't have to run. He couldn't run from things that got into his head. He was trapped into thought. He needed the poet to spring the trap.

Our earliest thinking probably had to do with the facts of the case. The sun shines and its warmth is good. Fire burns and wind and waters make noises. This root can be eaten. That root makes a man "stop." This "stopping" is what happens to the animals we hit in the hunt. What is it inside of us that dies when we do? Explainers were needed, and the man who stood aside was ready to talk.

In *Primitive Man as Philosopher,* an excellent little book which, unfortunately, has long been out of print (recently reissued as a paper back), Paul Radin points out that the origins of philosophic speculation in primitive and in early man are not to be found merely in the rude and dogmatic forms which religious beliefs took among the tribal groups. They are always the product and the interpretations of small intellectual classes, of the men who stood aside and observed. Their ideas, because of the limitations of their subject matter, may have been very crude, but they were always characterized by boldness, independence and freedom of thought, even within the limitations of their experience and their observation. They were far more tough-minded, far more realistic than they are usually given credit for being. Radin suggests, in fact that supernatural and magical practices and beliefs were of secondary value to them in the achievement of their practical aims. Yet, Radin writes, "The life of thought does not dominate and tyrannize over even the most intellectual of primitive people as it does over some of the least intellectual among us." [1] For primitive man, thoughts and words, acts and worths were and are considered as integral and concomitant elements. They are never considered separately nor is their import ever forgotten.

The universe is no riddle to a crab. It lives, eats and is finally

[1] Paul Radin, *Primitive Man as Philosopher,* New York: Appleton-Century, 1927, p. 59.

eaten. There are no questions in its life, only the simple declarative statements of existence. But questions have beleaguered the head and hand of man from his very beginnings. Man has none of the built-in computers of instinct. He learns only by doing and being done to, at first. Later he can get a lot of information at safe second hand. But then the questions come harder and more often. Some of the questions are just brute matters of fact, of what is going on. His healthy senses can get that kind of information for him. Some questions however just breed more questions and others deal with matters of practice, of what is more worth doing, and then the headaches start.

There is a deceptively friendly quality to questions. They seem to point to the area of experience in which their answers may be found. If you ask what time it is, you can't talk about the weather. But if you ask what is the good life, you may begin by talking about sewage disposal. By questions man catalogues his experience, focuses his attention on detail, establishes uniqueness, and destroys apparent order. Philosophers insist that all questions fall "naturally" under these headings: what is the nature of the world; what is the nature of man; what does it mean *to be;* what is goodness? Sometimes they are more subtle and frame the questions this way: what is knowing; what is value; what is existence? Whatever categories they use, any one of these questions will force the others to our attention and then we are back with O'Casey's characters asking about the stars.

We began asking ourselves and each other these questions long before there was any writing. They were old before we began to mark up cave walls. There was a rich oral literature concerning them before the written word made nonsense immortal. They are as old as myth, in fact they are its substance. Any story we write or tell, attempts, however obliquely, to come to grips with some of these questions. And now with almost fifty centuries of writing behind us it isn't at all surprising that we turn to books for the answers or the ways of answering our most persistent questions. Perhaps we don't turn immediately to "some treasured volume" or even to the man who owns one. Our ultimate recourse is not to books but to the tests of practicality. Yet these very tests are manageable insofar as we record their design and their use.

It is very important to know what in the world our world is like. What we say the world is, is determined in a large measure by how we behave in it. The very way we "see" things in this world is a consequence of how we learned to see. Some recent psychological experiments into the nature of perception are useful in explaining certain aspects of this kind of human behavior. *Life* Magazine, some years ago popularized some of these experiments with a picture essay of the so-called prepared house. This was an apparently "normal" dwelling in which "seeing was (not) believing." A six-foot man at one end of the living room appeared to be a giant, and at the other end a midget. Perspective lines, those most dependable of all measurers of distance for bifocal creatures, just didn't come together as they ought. Parallel lines were deceptively un-parallel and even the horizon beyond the window seemed to have gone askew. There is a story that one of the carpenters who worked on the project had a nervous breakdown when he found that he quite literally lost his way in the house he had helped to build. The story probably isn't true, but it serves to illustrate the dependency we have on things as they are. We can walk with confidence through our own darkened home, but we stumble along an empty unfamiliar alley.

We *learn* to see things, shapes, colors and relationships. We have successful experiences with them. We begin to accept what we "know" as the facts of life and we are thrown into a tizzy when any of these usual relationships are missing or altered. This explains in part our reluctance to accept new ideas about our world and our relation to it.

We have seen how books help to change the world. We have noted too, how books help to make change bearable, even reducing it on occasion to apparent unimportance. The clear sight of ancient prophets and the anguish of older sufferers stay alive in the book; family trees of men and nations are preserved between their covers. The life and times and dreams of any place echo from ancient scroll to modern microfilm. The poetry of Persia is now recorded on disc and tape, but the authority of the text is unassailed. The mirror we hold to nature is steadiest in our written literature. No matter how fast the rewind mechanism on a tape recorder is, it is still ephemeral stuff we hear.

With the coming of the revolutions in mass media we have learned to rely on sources of information other than the printed word. Yet film and recording, however permanent, have an ephemeral quality that makes them weaker than the cheapest, poorest printed page. So ultimately, even today, and for the foreseeable future, if we are to come to grips with meanings, it must be done on the field of the book. For example: there were for many years some highly successful cultural programs on radio, "The Town Meeting of the Air," "The American Forum," "Invitation to Learning," to name some of the outstanding ones. Very early in their careers, the producers of these programs found it wise and necessary to provide printed transcripts of their proceedings. Good talk doesn't always turn into good writing, in fact an accurate transcript of extempore remarks is often embarrassing to both speaker and listener, but the point to be demonstrated here is that the act of printing awards a dignity and an authority to the spoken word, as it always has.

While one phase of democracy, that of mass accessibility of information, is no more eminently demonstrated than in radio, television and the film, the other and infinitely more important aspect of this accessibility is to be found only where the selection, and control of time, place and pace is in the hands of the receiver, the reader. In film, radio and television, we are passive consumers with only the privilege of "take or leave it." How much and at what rate we get information or delight has been predetermined by some one or group who themselves are helpless once their creative effort has been achieved. It is true that the film or the recording may be "experienced" many times and each time something more may be learned, but the ideas and attitudes are fluid, they are always of the passing show, regardless of the number of times they pass. This is one of the major drawbacks of all of the so-called audio-visual aids in teaching. Unless they are ancillary to firm, purposive and directive teaching which is finally related to what is written down and spelled out, they are time fillers during which learning may easily be avoided.

Imagine, for example, as an adventure in ideas, the dialogue of Plato concerning the trial and death of Socrates. It could be read aloud before a camera with great eloquence but how closely could we follow its tightly knit argument? Imagine the Grand Inquisitor passage from *The Brothers Karamazov*; it can easily be made to come alive before microphone and camera, but what would happen to its awful, anguished periods? They would crawl by us, inexorably at a speaker's pace, though our minds might scream for a pause to reflect or to taste the full measure of fear and hope, or to rush ahead to gain a fuller view of the huge ideas. Consider the Constitution of the United States as it was "brought to life" and explained by an eminent jurist. The performance was moving and even instructive, as a good sermon might be, but unless it led back to books, it could never be any more than this.

No, for the persistent questions that man asks and for the answers he has tried to give and take he needs the persistent page of the book. Try to understand the universe! A colored cartoon might be of some help, an animated graph might lead the unskilled mind through the mazes of motion. Photographs of the dark reaches between the stars might thrill us with their frozen silences. The drama of the creation hypotheses might be told with moving models. But a little book like Fred Hoyle's brilliantly written *Nature of the Universe* can do more in a few hours than any gimmicked display we are yet capable of rigging, to stimulate interest, to instruct and to challenge thought.

Is it presumptuous to ask what is the nature of the universe? Some people think so, some people have always thought so. This is usually because they believe that they know its nature and want to preserve a trade or family secret. What we say things are affects what we do with them and about them. If the universe is huge, oppressive, inscrutable, unfathomable, then nothing can be known, nothing can be said, not a thing can be done about it. But this sort of description is always given by someone to someone else, indicating a kind of knowledge that sets the knower apart from the commonality. He may be a priest, a scholar, a poet or a politician; he is often all of these at once. He seeks to protect us from our own untrained curiosity. He wishes to be our ears and eyes and mind. He will say, as Santayana said, "It is not wisdom to be only wise,/ And on the inward vision close the eyes,/ But it is wisdom to believe the heart." This is the philosopher as poet, warning the rest of us away from the domain of thought, for our own good, of course.

There is no "idle curiosity." Knowing something makes a difference. In fact, it makes us different. When the world was "known" to be nothing more than a rim of land around the Mediterranean Sea, man located his enterprises within its scope. As soon as he entertained the possibility that there was more to the world, there was more, and the Phoenicians breached the Gates of Hercules. So long as the earth was the center of the universe, the stars were tiny lights, only just out of reach. But knowledge is a hunger-maker. Our appetite for facts is boundless and our appetites for explanations are sated only in action which ends in another kind of question.

We may begin by asking what the world is, but even before we have worked out much of an answer, we rush on to another, "more important" question. We want to know more about ourselves. In some ways this kind of a question shakes our world more profoundly than the first one. "Tell me," we ask, "was ever a man so fortunate (or so sore beset) as I?" This is another way of asking, "Am I alone?" And we seek out the answers with our minds full of corollary questions. Job asked them, and even the Voice in the Whirlwind stuttered. How indeed can we account for the presence of evil in the world? What is evil, anyway? Just to begin to answer these questions puts us in the position of admitting and accepting the existence of a force or essence that suffuses acts we describe as evil, and of identifying the content of those acts as undesirable. This represents no great intellectual difficulty. The tests for the presence of evil are pretty reliable. John Donne put it simply when he described it as "that which diminishes any man." But when we attempt to account for the presence of evil, we are in the position of Job who tries to understand how it is possible for a just and good God to sanction it. Even an attempt to escape the dilemma by using a naturalistic explanation doesn't succeed. The question persists. One way of attempting to circumvent the problem is to suggest that when man "arrived on the scene" or emerged from animality, he with his power of "rational" thought saw better and more efficient ways of doing things, whereupon the older ways became "evils." But this, the religious will insist, misses the point entirely. Surely more efficient ways of doing things are better than wasteful methods. There is no denying the absolute superiority of flush toilets over the slit-trench. Evil is not a mere "mistake." The old Greek error is here compounded. Their word for "sin" simply means missing the mark. Evil is the expression of the way man manages his relations with his fellows to his or their detriment. Sin is the index of the level of his awareness of his perversity. Such definitions would be acceptable to very few moralists and almost no theologians and they are offered here—not for defense—but to demonstrate the way we can move in our questions from the cosmological to the commonplace and how in practical affairs the latter present by far the greater challenge.

In times of trouble, or more accurately when we are troubled about the times in which we live, we seek comfort, solace and strength from any information that we can find about past predicaments. A father suffering his son's adolescent bull-headedness, when he reads across fifty centuries that a Babylonian boy caused similar anguish, may smile a little, and feel far safer than had he only to depend upon the clear scientific statements of some child guidance counselor. A young wife in her new husband's strange community may read of Ruth in the alien corn and learn that troubles need not be disasters. A man stopped in mid-career by the awful emptiness of mere achievement may be refreshed by a novelist's exploration of the mind of another man with a similar problem. Anyone puzzled by his or her own private uniqueness may find in

a study of human experience and behavior, a realization that difference need not be considered a disaster. One may be alone without
being forsaken. One may be troubled or triumphant. The grandest
plans may go stale before use. The immortality of youth will be
stolen by ten thousand paltry days and yet no thing is wholly lost.
Whatever the nature of the questions that plague us, whatever the
fears that beset our nights, the renewing magic of the book is always
close at hand.

There is a lot of worshipful nonsense that is written about this
magic. This is the fee that we pay to our other selves. This is our
quitrent of man's estate. The mountain of print on which we stand
raises us towards the receding stars and flattens the near horizons.
Someone sometimes somewhere has struggled with the questions
even as we do. Whether in trivial novel, timeless poem, or garrulous,
ink-stained diary, someone has wondered as we wonder and tried to
mine useful answers from the hard-rock record of past experience.
The soul-shaping literary experience is not only the province of the
man of letters. We all have had it, often. Remember the book you
read to tatters? Recall that story that was so right that it dissolved
all your troubles? Remember those books that you read at the end
of childhood. We promise ourselves that we will read them again,
but we never do. We say we must search for them again, but we
carefully put it off. Some of these treasures are best kept in distant
memory. The child's eye has a vision we all must lose. But there
are other books.

Compare the best seller list of today with that of a generation ago.
In January 1930 *All Quiet on the Western Front* led the fiction list.
Today it is *Andersonville*. In 1930 *Henry the Eighth* led the general
list; today it is *The Spy Who Came in from the Cold*. Second on
the general list in 1930 was Ernest Dimnet's *The Art of Thinking*.
Walter Lippmann's *Preface to Morals* was third. Others were Will
Durant's *Mansions of Philosophy*, Claude Bowers' *The Tragic Era*
and Eugene O'Neill's *Strange Interlude*. We are reading all about
The Naked Society, Profiles in Courage and *My Years with General
Motors*. On the fiction list of the 1930's was *White Oaks of Jalna*,

by de la Roche, Ellen Glasgow's *They Stooped to Folly* and *Dodsworth,* by Sinclair Lewis.

These lists are more than the index of the publisher's ability to sell his wares, although they are pre-eminently that. They also bespeak our abiding concern with certain kinds of questions. It is not a very difficult task to show parallels between literary preferences and public fears, but it would be both daring and dishonest to claim any unique connection. Then as now we were interested in what happened before our time. Historical fiction and non-fiction are equally to be found on both lists. Then as now we were concerned with the birth and growth of ideas, made palatable in popular prose.

We pore over the record of old yesterdays to find greater fools and more perfidious villains than we know. We tell ourselves that there is order and method in the workings of our minds. We catalogue our morals, we lay bare our peccadilloes, we sing songs and remember quiet times, and we hope. That hope makes us see similarities and resemblances even where they do not exist; sometimes most especially where they do not exist. Consider the tendency implicit in the examination of these two lists. "Neither better nor worse" is implied. We say this to secure present assurance.

Hesiod, writing about the time of Homer in his *Theogony* cries, "Would that I had not been born in this age, but either before or after it!" In the Golden Age long before his time, the first gods under Cronus created a Golden Race, a wondrous people living almost as the gods themselves, neither toiling nor suffering, for whom a long-deferred death was only a painless sleep. Tiring of such near perfection the gods then made a Silver Race with a century long youth, sudden maturity accompanied by suffering and quick death. Then Zeus came and created a Brazen Race, made for fighting each other, a quick harvest for black Death. Zeus then touched by poetry, tried again and produced the Heroic Race which fought at Thebes and Troy. For them death was a passport to the Isles of the Blest. The last product of the god's toil was the meanest and the worst, the Iron Race, possessing few virtues and all of the vices of the human spirit. They were connivers, they were corrupt, they dishonored each other and their parents for good measure. They made war meanly and for pecuniary reasons. They bought and sold everything, were impious and stingy even to the gods themselves. They were in fact, enough like us to be our ancestors. They were.

"There were giants in those days!" Hesiod whined. The golden days have gone before us. There are no heroes any more and life is flavored with bitter earth. Tomorrow is a tunnel of darkness with a yawning pit at the far end. Let us sit quietly and recall the old stories of the greater times that cannot come again. There were Hesiod-minded people a thousand years before Troy burned brightly in the shadow of the wooden horse. The mark of Hesiod touches the pen of today's poet who talks about the world ending in a whimper and of another who would prefer to be "a worm in a dried apple than a son of man."

Art is the great pruner. It cuts away all ugliness and all that is ordinary, making each age, however squalid, a candidate for the golden cloak. How amazed would Hesiod have been to see the label golden applied to his poor time. How dumfounded would the serf have been, living in muck with well-fed rats, beside the cathedral close, to discover that he was flourishing in a sun-drenched time of golden glory. Aren't you, who have lived past childhood, a little surprised to find that the 1920's possessed the magic sheen, that the arts were more virile then, the theatre richer, the novel full of achieved promise, and the commonwealth in general purposive, certain and secure?

This attitude may be one aspect of art in motion but it has also been called Primitivism which is a little unfair to most primitive peoples. It can better be applied as it is used to describe these so-called primitive art works of uneducated people like Grandma Moses, George Kane and the nineteenth-century French painter, Rousseau. It is a drive toward simplifying, an impatience with structure, a distrust of complex order and in a way a refusal to accept the responsibilities of difficult contemporary thinking. And yet this way of reading the aspects of the human enterprise is neither dishonest nor invalid. It is one way of getting a more distant view, of getting perspective, trying, as Socrates did, to "see life steady and see it whole."

Francis Bacon, writing with confidence in the dawn of the modern age announced that he would take all knowledge as his province. He could and did. He was probably one of the last men to be able to do so. Aristotle, long before him could compass the range of human knowledge and Bacon's Renaissance gentlemen contemporaries could do likewise. They were the last of the great amateur generalizers. The rumbling and clatter of the printing press played counterpoint to the tool-noises of laboratory and work-shop. Investigation and inquiry were being teamed up with the old Roman bookkeeping system and the results were published, in a slow trickle at first and then in an ever swelling word-flood and the intellectual sons of Francis Bacon had to become specialists if they were to know anything at all well enough to put it to use. In the process science itself had to become almost anti-intellectual, forsaking philosophy, which demands an ultimate commitment to social use, in order to achieve that uninvolved "objectivity" without which the scientist could not come to grips with the reports of his senses, his tools and his tables.

This apparent contradiction, the avoidance of the social commitment in order to be useful, caused and still causes many a scientist to split his personality. Today he is trying to sew up that split. What happens in his laboratory helps and hurts people. He can no longer be a profligate father. He has the responsibility of housebreaking his brain children. But philosophy, the old queen of the sciences has all along remained as housekeeper, tidying up, mending and preserving all those things the men-folk either neglected or forgot how to use. She kept in touch with the old family friend, the poet and with those noisy and haughty relations, religion and politics, and among them they kept in touch with the problems of truth, goodness and beauty until such a time as the men with the measuring rods would come back into the parlor.

Bookkeeping is essential in counting house and workshop. You can tell the worth of things by adding up costs in money spent and energy expended and subtracting this from what you get for what you do. You can even assign money values to "intangibles" like goodwill and morale. You can convert real risks to fiduciary fictions, translate those into money terms, interpolate cash for credit and the old enemy chance becomes the raw material of the insurance business. Divide responsibility and multiply security. Perhaps there were giants in the Golden Days, but had they the sense to underwrite themselves, they could not have been liquidated at the whim of any god. A seat on an exchange is more stable than a throne on Olympus.

We must distinguish between bookkeeping and the keeping of books; the former is a generally successful method of controlling or at least recording short term events, the latter is the conservation of all that we have ever suffered, endured and thought. The reading of a column of figures tells us nothing if this is all we read, but the substance of all other kinds of writings, whether they be water commissioner's reports on the rising of the Nile in the spring of 4000 B.C. or the remarks of a terrified poet watching a spider trap a fly is the substance of the only real racial memory we will ever possess. It is through the use of this kind of written memory that we learn from the experiences of others. It is out of this that we phrase those questions that help us build things better than we found them. Let us look at these questions again:

Suppose we say, "I don't understand. Please tell me what the world is all about." We are asking at least two kinds of questions. We want to know what makes water run downhill; what makes stars shine; what makes grass grow. Out of such kinds of questions science is born and grows. We might also be asking why things happen in the way they do. This is the search for causes. It is implied in the other questions. It is made explicit in these. The attempted explanations produce philosophy or art or a mixture of both. We are rather easily satisfied with answers to the first kind of questions. The factual description of a process is enough. The explanation of a sequence of steps in growth or development is sufficient even where full understanding isn't reached. We often read highly technical reports and come away with at least the assurance that there is some "natural" or scientific, or at any rate a reliable set of explanations for what has happened. To this category belong the host of semi-scientific and popular books and articles about the nature of the world and its works. This kind of reading eases the pique of curiosity. It gives us the feeling that we are "in the know." It is at least a partial explanation of the persistence on the best seller lists or at least a very high level of sales of such books as *The Sea Around Us* by Rachel Carson and the continuing popularity in the paperbacks of the books of George Gamow, the physicist, *The Birth and Death of the Sun, The Autobiography of the Earth, One, Two, Three, Infinity,* etc., and a host of other titles on geology, physics, chemistry, astronomy, etc.

The phenomenon of the widespread publication and reprint of competent, brilliant and often very difficult works of non-fiction in the paper covered books hasn't begun to be evaluated. Ruth Benedict's *Patterns of Culture* and Margaret Mead's *Coming of Age in Samoa* and *Sex and Temperament in Six Savage Societies*—both rather technical books, directed to the student of cultural anthropology—have sold and continue to sell far more today in paper covered reprints than they did in the original trade editions.

These books demand a lot from the reader. They were not written for a popular market, and yet the popular market has claimed them. There is of course the attraction of exotic sexual practices and the potent vicarious experience one can get even from an objective, scientific discussion of the kinds of behavior that are taboo in our culture. This to a considerable degree is the explanation of the wide popularity of Kinsey's first book. The behavior there discussed would cause the banning of any novel but there is far more here than venal curiosity. We want to be reassured about the scope and nature of human behavior. We want to know that our private thoughts and secret practices are not so frighteningly unique as to withdraw us from the company of our fellow men. It is not necessary to our purpose that we fully understand what is being examined.

It is sufficient that we get hints and clues that large groups of other people have thought and acted as we have. In a way a sin that is shared widely enough is not so desperate an occasion. And the penance of torturing the conscience is less severe. But more important, whatever we learn about the varieties and range of human behavior, from novel, travel book or scientific report, the deeper our understanding of ourselves and our fellows can become.

We seek and desire uniformities; that way lies security too, but the greatest and continuing challenge comes from the apparent conflict in values and value claims. These exist between one generation and another, between one nation and another and between human cultures whenever they are in contact. We hold property to be sacred, expendable only under duress. The wastrel and the prodigal has been the butt of our literature from its beginnings but there are people for whom property is a consumer item, designed for conspicuous use. The man who handsomely wastes his substance is held in highest esteem. We would put such a man in a mental hospital. In some cultures a husband will offer the convenience of his wife to a wayfaring stranger. We would call him cuckold and arrest the others as adulterers. For us, the bride wears white; for others, it is the funereal color. For us, the aging father is gently succored, for others, the son is remiss in his filial duty if he doesn't kill the old man.

Thrift, responsibility, faithfulness, industry, integrity, respect, deference, humility, cooperation; around the ideas represented by such words our values cluster, but we measure them against competition, aggressiveness, leadership, control and all the positive forms of acquisitive behavior that characterize so-called free men in a so-called productive society. Here are the sources of most of our ulcers and all of our anguish. This is what the existentialist describes as the condition of despair, anguish and aloneness. Man is unique, single and solitary. We think of this as the source of dignity. Some societies and some members of our society act on the assumption that it is the source of disease. Only the mass has character, only the state has personality, only by losing our identity in the infinite can we save ourselves from the terror of solitude.

These notions are strange to us on the printed page. They would be utterly repugnant to most of us in experience. We could not "take them"; we couldn't manage them. But knowing of them, vicariously, they are susceptible to control, their dangerous potency is reduced to manageable proportions. All of the great and base emotions which we are capable of experiencing only to our peril, we can survive with comfort and profit between the covers of a book.

Aristotle wrote wisely about the uses of tragedy as an intellectual and emotional cleansing agent, as catharsis. To participate at safe second hand in the decline and degradation of some high and noble personality who suffers from a fatal flaw of character that only we can see, acts like some drugs; therapeutic in small doses but deadly at full strength. To actually be Mrs. Loman in Miller's *Death of a Salesman* is a disaster; to see and understand her suffering brings a measure of wisdom and a fragment of peace that Willy earned the hard way. But even to "assist" at a play, and the French use of the word is appropriate here, can be stronger meat than some of us can digest. The printed text gives us more control. We can "go gently into that good-night," or we can wallow unashamed and alone in the depths of despondency, or we can "stop by the woods" in the quiet pulse of thought.

We read to learn. We read to live another way. We read to quench some blind and shocking fire. We read to weigh the worth of what we have done or dare to do. We read to share our awful secrets with someone we know will not refuse us. We read our way into the presence of great wisdom, vast and safe suffering, or into the untidy corners of another kind of life we fear to lead. With the book we can sin at a safe distance. With Maugham's artist in *The Moon and Sixpence,* we can discommit ourselves of family responsibility and burn our substance and our talent in bright colors on a tropic isle. But this is no child's play. In this kind of reading there is profit and loss and to take the one and sustain the other our prior investments in psychological and intellectual securities must have been considerable and sound. Our maturity rating must be high enough to warrant the title *adult*.

Mature reading is more than and different from the mere application of the basic skills of "reading" that were discussed in the preceding chapter. It requires, of course, the cultivation of an ever growing vocabulary, in fact of several different though essentially related vocabularies. It requires some minimum level of physical well-being. It requires an ability to "shift gears," that is, to suit the way we read to what we read. Certainly a short story in a mass-circulation magazine neither requires nor deserves the attention we would give to one by Thomas Mann, Joseph Conrad, Sherwood Anderson or Katherine Mansfield. We would not study a sports column with the same intensity that we must bring to Albert Schweitzer's testament of faith. We don't read a cake recipe the way we read instructions on an income tax form. So, the adult must be able to read with discrimination as to the methods by which he reads. More especially he must be aware of the purposes for which he reads.

The same piece of writing may be read at many different levels, regardless of the author's obvious intent. If we choose to read for amusement, for recreation, for what is loosely now called escape, we should be able to do so, whether the writer be Plato or Mickey Spillane. This may shock some people's sensibilities, but it is hardly sensible to be so easily shocked. The book can be an instrument of widely different usage. It can be as fine and precise as a scalpel or as blunt and gross as a pole axe. Its service changes as we tell ourselves why we read.

Why ever we read, there are certain conditions that are present when we read as adults. We must be aware of all of them to some degree. For in the first place, an author is speaking to us. The child and the immature person is rarely aware that anyone is behind the book. We may avoid, if that is our purpose, any concern with the author's intent, even if he announces it loudly either in preface or in style. In the second place, even in the attitude of "escape," we work with our reading. We bring to bear upon the act of reading all that we are in terms of experience, all that we know, all that we are capable of feeling. Present at all times are clusters of attitudes, preconceptions, prejudices and preferences concerning the meanings of words and ideas. A white resident of Alabama cannot read Lillian Smith's *Strange Fruit* in quite the same way as a Philadelphia Quaker will read it. A labor leader won't read *The Legend of Henry Ford* by Keith Sward in quite the same way that a dedicated member of the Optimist Clubs might. A clergyman could not read Homer W. Smith's *Man and His Gods* with anything approaching the equanimity of a confirmed atheist.

A third condition that is present whenever we read as adults, is really a corollary to the second. It is a kind of transaction between the writer and the reader. Although the author is done with his writing, he continues to work on the mind of each new or renewed reader. Marya Dmitievna in *War and Peace* never enters twice in the same way the room at the Rostov's dinner party—but her vitality, her boisterous aliveness, is always there for any reader. The way a reader feels when he reads and the conditions under which he reads, physical as well as psychological, all contribute to how he reads. This is more apparent in poetry with its concentrated compass but it is present in all forms of writing to some degree. Tolstoy has made Marya available, it is the reader who makes her live, and she will be alive differently for different readers and even for the same reader at different times. What we are and what we are living through at a particular time reworks what we read and makes it a unique experience fraught with new meanings that we never suspected. In the fall of 1941, Matthew Arnold's lines from "Dover Beach" referred to something he could never have known: ". . . on the French coast the light/ Gleams and is gone; the cliffs of England stand,/ Glimmering and vast, out in the tranquil bay." They will always have a particular quality for those who lived through World War II. For others who came before or after, these lines will have different and perhaps less-potent meanings.

A fourth condition which is present in the reading of all but the most abstract of technical writing is that mature reading provides and even requires a *living through* an experience, not merely getting knowledge *about* a real or imagined happening. We actually come *with* Isak in Knut Hamsun's *Growth of the Soil,* into the strange and desolate new country and, depending on our abilities as readers, we sense some of his feelings and taste some of his unspoken hopes. This is more and different from the adolescent identification of a boy or girl who has been picked up by some powerfully written story in the delight of helpless suffering or joy, and carried to some seeming world-shattering conclusion. The mature reader is past most seduction but is not blasé. In working with the author he may be learning something new in the experience but he is also in a measure, controlling the shape of that experience. He has to accept the fact of the fiction but he need not either love or hate what he sees. In some ways he participates in the growth of the characters he is reading about. He takes the hints and suggestions of the author and amalgamates them with the substance of his own actual and vicarious experiences giving a flesh-and-blood roundness to the creatures of the writer's fancy.

These conditions then, the readers awareness of the presence of the author, the reader working with the author, the pressure of current experience and the reader's ability and necessity to *live through* the constructed characters and events, all combine to direct and to color the aspects of every particular act of reading.

But maturity in reading goes far beyond this. In fact these conditions, by themselves, do not add up to the total act of reading. For, whatever we read, be it a mail-order catalogue or a treatise on the gods, we integrate it with the continuing flow of experiences and dealings that is our life. The theme to which we have returned so often in this book, is that through the writings of others, past and contemporary, we are able to live so richly in so short a time.

Very few of us are theoretical mathematicians and almost none of us are geniuses in that field, but Norbert Weiner allows us, in his autobiographical volumes *Ex-Prodigy* and *I Am a Mathematician,* to be a little bit of both. Few of us can die more than once and fewer still can afford the emotional and intellectual expense of any long-term consideration of the prospect, but the poets and philosophers for thousands of years have made this necessary luxury available for a modest down payment of thought and fear. In our complex society we cannot afford the power and the patience of learning a great deal about a very little, but there are always some who do give their life to the study of a fly or the death of a distant star or the memory of an ancient accident. From these and others we can live and learn whole lifetimes in a matter of rather easy hours.

Yet integration is not enough. Meaning and understanding are necessary to thought. They are not sufficient. To think, as we have already noted, requires that we do something to ourselves and our surroundings, with what we have learned. We have to make judgments about these matters and act upon them too. Unless we change our attitudes and behaviors, we are not thinking. This change may be a more secure holding to what we know or believe. It might well be an outright rejection of what we do or read. It will usually be some kind of modification. These judgments and their consequent actions are made against the total background of our experiences and our attitudes. They are the indicators of criticism at work.

Criticism is the most subtle and pervasive aspect of the reader thinking. The kinds of questions we ask ourselves about what we read, the ways in which we interpret the tapestry of meaning that we find upon the page, the methods and manners by which we relate what has gone before to what is going on, the decisions we make about accepting or refusing to accept the author's arrangement of facts or his declaration of viewpoint, all of this is the raw material of criticism. And all of this is prior to any esthetic judgment we may eventually make. Esthetic judgment comes out of contemplation, a relatively quiet thinking through of what we have gone through. It is the balancing and weighing of what we can see and know about the relationships of the elements of the total reading experience we have had and how these square with the independent attitudes and understandings we originally brought to this reading. Sometimes, perhaps most often, this contemplation is indicated by little more than a grunt of satisfaction or a monosyllable of disapproval, but whether it is only this or a great deal more it provides the motive power for any thinking or doing that comes out of the reading experience. It is out of the strength we develop in this pause-in-thought that we gain the capacity to say what anything is worth.

The one aspect of mature reading that appears most obvious and immediate is the difference we feel within ourselves as a consequence of this reading. This may be trivial as the matter of having read one more book or as great as a turn-about in political belief or religious conviction. It is in fact a reconstruction of ourselves. For the reading that is purposive results in a rebuilding, a reorganizing of some of the patterns of our thought and our personality. Just as some books have changed the world, some can change our minds. All reading has a polyp-like effect of change by tiny additions. This last is a far more modest claim than it appears to be. It is like saying that the longer you live, the more you use words, the more varied your experience with words becomes. It is our experience with ideas and with concepts which are expressed in words, whether they are articulated or not, that ultimately makes the difference that reconstructs our thinking and acting. To become aware of and to accept the social and psychological implications of "do unto others . . ." as an injunction rather than as a slogan requires a specific change in behavior as well as in attitude.

The kind of reading we have been discussing and labeling as "mature" is the only kind out of which we can develop useful answers to meaningful questions, but the act of reading would be a drab affair if it were entirely this. Christopher Morley suggested long ago that "Heaven must be a place where you can sit down and laugh." The enjoyment of laughter both the internal chuckle and the erupting guffaw is a social act that usually requires the presence of more than one person. It forces us to move from books to people more quickly than any other kind of reading. We wish to share what we have experienced. But there are the private jokes between us and the books we read, about the world. There we need distance, and time to savor the comic element.

The film, radio and television do not permit this. We have only the control of self denial, of abstention. But it is a waste of time to contrast or compare the book with these media. Essentially, there is no real competition here. The only skill that is fully shared is that of attention and even here listening to a film or television differs from that of radio and in none of these is the quality of attention possible that one can bring to the printed word. One thing ought to be recognized however, and that is the fact that these media have largely taken the place of light and some so-called escape fiction. Although mystery and Western fans might object, it is plain one can get one's "kicks" with far less effort by viewing or listening. This is not to deny a certain kind of excellence found only in books, but merely to say that for many people, the effort of reading is reserved for more meaty fare. This extends as well into the field of journalism. The quality of newspaper reporting has changed considerably since the birth of radio and yet, do we look to the morning newspaper for the headline news we got the night before? We can be and usually are far more selective in that kind of reading and the modern newspaperman provides us with background material which in detail and understanding far surpass the best reporting of fifty years ago. The large metropolitan newspapers, with a very few obvious exceptions perform an educative function of greater value today than at any time in their histories. A modern reporter needs a nose for news but he must have a mind able to discern relationships between events, perceptive enough to see them in their social and historical sequences.

But for all this the reading fare of maturity is neither a dull nor a somber affair. The great questions are there to be tested against a wide range of experience. The joys are richer. Books can be mined beyond the depths of their authors' design. The universe may still be infinite but it is not unfathomable. The varieties of human experience reach far beyond use and wont, beyond the invention of novelist or poet, but such knowledge diminishes only our parochial distrust of man's possibilities. The ancient mysteries of mind and body are lifted from their magical haze, and psyche is joined to soma to make man more whole and wholesome than the doom-seeking divines ever thought possible. The kinds of knowledges that are available and understandable to the book reading mind, may not return us to the fancied universal knowledge of Francis Bacon, but we can gain an ability to deal with larger and more clearly related generalizations than he could comprehend. The physicist and psychologist can talk to each other and we can listen and understand. Though we may be terrified by our capacity for destruction, this terror is tempered by a realization, however dim, that we can and are, building the better world that was the fabric of yesterday's dreams.

This is neither poppycock nor prayerful Pollyannaism. This is long-sighted fact. For despite the confusion and the conflict that are so characteristic of our age, despite the recognition that war is endemic with us, despite low pressure thinking at the highest levels of government, we are possessed also of profound insights and perceptive knowledge of the nature of the human enterprise. The curse of Babel has not yet been lifted, but "the charm is wound up" and we know something of how it works. We may no longer be devout believers in some arcane power called Progress. In some ways we are as fearful of the encroachment of the machine upon our life as our fathers were. We have come to accept the enlargement of our leisure with little awareness of its possibilities for us as a source of mental as well as physical health. We are becoming a hobby-ridden nation in certain respects. We are reading more instructional materials than ever before. Men and women tackle complicated home jobs successfully that only recently they would have given to professionals. We are becoming good tinkerers and in tinkering, success comes easily and is easy to recognize.

As Lester Asheim in his chapter "What Do Adults Read" points out:

So long as "action" seems more desirable in our society than thought, it is going to be difficult to promote reading as a socially desirable activity. So long as rewards from any time-consuming activity must be tangible and immediate, it is going to be difficult to convince more than a few in our society that reading has a justifiable claim upon their time. So long as reading is difficult to do, it is going to suffer in competition with less difficult activities. These are formidable barriers to breach, but there is one weapon which suggests itself in every one of these instances. That weapon is education, and while it is not—in the most literal sense of the words—fool-proof, it is the most promising one we have.[2]

The adult reader of books is a distinct member of a distinguished minority in this country. Studies, such as the one above are sobering and even a little frightening. Less than thirty per cent of our total population may be considered "active" readers in the sense implied here. The professional man tends to *use* books that are specifically helpful in his work. These are glorified "do-it-yourself" tomes which show him how to think what other people have thought. He is too often without a thought of his own, like the ghost of Kipling's "Tomlinson" from whom the devils "threshed a stock of print and book, and winnowed the chattering wind,/And many a soul where-from he stole, but his we cannot find."

It is exciting, as we have said, to see the great success of the paper-backed book. It is less than consoling to find, in a recent Gallup Poll that three-quarters of those little books, of all titles, are bought by only ten per cent of our population. When an executive book club was started, it floundered badly because, it was discovered, not more than twenty per cent of executives would read as many as a dozen books a year dealing with general subjects, even in their own profession. Most of their reading was of the "practical" type which they deemed essential to their success. When the club quit its program of offering books of "lasting value" and switched to "do-it-yourself" manuals for junior executives, it became a successful business.

The businessman, the labor leader, the teacher too, tend to *use* those books that seem to assure some immediate returns on the reading investment. An important book on some historical subject

[2] Lester B. Asheim, "What Do Adults Read?" in Nelson B. Henry, Editor, *Reading*, the Fifty-Fifth Yearbook of the University of the National Society for the Study of Education, University of Chicago Press, 1956, Part II, p. 28.

for example, rarely reaches them, or anyone else for that matter. A study of the best eight "histories," so judged by a jury of over a hundred scholars, found that the *total* sales for these eight books was less than four thousand, which means that not even all the colleges and universities managed to get copies. This is another case of specialists writing for specialists. It would be interesting to ask if the historians who read these history books found time for other books of "lasting value."

The job, as Asheim said, is one for education of a kind and a quality we have hardly dared envision. Our leisure is increasing, although many of us try to smother it under a mountain of "busy-work."

The adventure in ideas that many of us glimpsed in our early youth, is still waiting to be embarked upon. It is true that "action seems more desirable than thought" to many of us and that the rewards of thought cannot be seen as clearly as a well-mowed lawn. It is true that for too many of us reading is very hard work, that it is not amenable to any of the electronic labor saving devices that have made radio and television such inexpensive joys. "Hope" is offered in that direction by a do-it-yourself kit for the building of a reading-rate accelerator. It is a portable gadget that quite literally pushes the nose down the page faster than we are in the habit of going. But that is a false hope. The only reading rate accelerator that really will work is much more expensive. It costs time. It costs thought. It costs the investment in ideas, the extension of intellectual appetites. It requires the stretching of our emotional range. It is hard work at first. After a while it can become a cherished necessity. For the world will grow larger again and the actions of man and nature will seem to acquire meanings we thought they had lost. That accelerator is the rusty little interest we carry around inside ourselves; an interest in man and his works; an interest in the why and the how of things; an interest in the living self we call by our own name.

The Great Books Foundation tries to help people put this accelerator into operation and to date they have been hugely unsuccessful precisely because they themselves have fallen victims to the cult of the ready-mix and the instant pudding. In effect they have been offering these riches on the installment plan, a little time down, the rest in tiny, predigested installments. They trained "leaders" to lead discussions about "great" ideas. They culled the "total" intellectual heritage of the Western world, and sampled the product of the East, and presented some snippets in pamphlet form for those who would buy intellectual health and freedom at discount rates. For the financially braver souls, they offer a handsomely bound and printed set for about $250. The program and the books have a certain snob appeal. The set is well within the tradition of conspicuous consumption. It takes up a yard and a half of wall space and, with the proper encyclopedia, it presents a formidable posture of sterile intellectuality.

Great books of great ideas are all around us. They are being written at this moment. But books become great as they have impact upon living minds. A jury of scholars may nominate "obvious" titles and have their candidates accepted by pleasing pluralities. The book that counts is the one that shakes your ideas into clearer focus and leads you to other books and eventually to more effective ways of thinking and seeing things and events and the relations among them. A home library cannot be bought under the direction of an interior decorator. The only interior to be decorated is your own mind. Your library grows only with garden care. You are proud at first of any sprout, but the weeds come as soon as your taste and experience tell you what the weeds are. Then the library begins to be the seedbed of ideas with a promise of nourishing the whole family. It need not be a big plot, a few hundred books will do. Many of the titles can be started from the little paperbacks. When you have relearned how to make a book your own, you can go on to the more permanent bindings.

It is tempting to offer a list here, but then we would be repeating the mistake of the Great Books. Use any personal motivation of interest that is at hand. Don't begin with any grand notions of picking up the skeins of lost romance and youth. There is still much "growing up" to be done. Start by reading regularly, any kind of book. Read one a week. Read *about* books, and begin to be selective. Vary the fiction with general titles in areas of your interest and within six months deliberately shift to more meaty writing. In every field of human knowledge there are now books that offer a dependable and highly readable survey of the major ideas, practices and discoveries in that field. These can become your source books for further reading. As in all learning, and learning is what you will be doing a great deal of, it grows upon itself and becomes easier and more delightful because of that growth. Follow these interests as long as they are exciting but vary your reading, learn, as we try to teach children today, to shift gears in your reading. Read for pleasure, for relaxation, for escape, just as much as you read for any more "presentable" reason. Don't be reluctant to talk about the ideas that excite you. It is not really very hard to find someone to listen to you. Don't chase after the biggest ideas, but don't shy away from them when they confront you. There is a kind of magic here, but there is no mystery.

Walt Whitman knew this:

Books are to be called for and supplied on the assumption that the process of reading is not half-sleep, but in the highest sense an exercise, a gymnastic struggle; that the reader is doing something for himself.

10

Youth Reads for What?

Note to the teacher concerning the boy in the back of the room:

He sits in front of you every day, his shiny red hair carefully piled, twisted and swirled into a belligerent pompadour, his pug nose astride a grinning face. He outwits every trick you dream up to catch a shred of his interest. He won't read aloud even if you don't call it a recitation. He culls his "book reports" from dust jackets or cribs them from friends. The achievement test you gave him at the beginning of the year placed him three grades below in vocabulary and four below in comprehension. He spells with an inventive abandon that even Chaucer would have envied. During the writing periods you are lucky if you squeeze a dozen lines out of him. They are usually about some battle between the Martians and the Terrestrians over the possession of some uranium-rich asteroid or about using a space-warp to reach the fifth planet of Aldebaran. When the rest of the class is "reading" he either drums with a pencil on the desk or reproduces a battle of the "space-rats," complete with disruptive sound-effects.

Red won't read. The evidence says he can't. Your experience backs up the evidence. You have got to get him into the ninth grade next year. The guidance counselor says he can't take a third year in the eighth. But he can't read. How can you face Miss Leigh who has troubles enough with the decline and fall of culture in this unhappy land?

There is something you ought to know. The "evidence" is wrong. So are you. Red is reading under your nose and behind your back. He is reading with anguish and purpose and eagerness, and he is scared stiff that you may discover it. He knows you won't approve. That bulge on his hip is a paperback with the cover ripped off. You and every other teacher in the school have sworn to uphold the principal's principle that the "filthy trash" must be destroyed. Remember the teacher's bulletin

149

on March 14? "It has come to our attention that there is an *outbreak* of the reading of questionable literature in paperbacked form especially among the boys. It is our responsibility to the parents and the community, to see that none of this material remains on school property." No titles were mentioned of course. That would only increase their sales at the newstand. But you've never suspected Red even as a guilty reader. Or have you?

He is caught up in the hotrod craze, you know that of course. You tore up three of those magazines last week. The only teacher he "works for" is Mr. Wales, in the Science Club. He spends hours after school with that silly business of grinding a telescope lens. He plans to use it late this summer to study the approach of Mars. Miss Thomas says he always gets his algebra in late and wrong. But he is working out the focal length of that lens to a thousandth of an inch.

You see, Red is reading three kinds of material, all very important to him, one possibly very shocking to you, none of which he can find or keep in a "legitimate" classroom. Of course the class is a big one. They seem to be getting bigger every year and the kids are so different from each other that it is a constant struggle to keep them all working at the same textbooks. And the paperwork keeps piling up. If only the children would read quietly for an hour in the morning it would not be so hard—but Red starts them off, and you can't send him down to the office every day.

Here is a suggestion. It may be dangerous, but remember back in your student days when you agreed with the professor that teaching is a dangerous profession? Start with the hip pocket. It may mean choosing loyalty to the interest of a child over loyalty to an ill-considered bulletin. The worst that can happen to you is a reprimand, the best that can happen to Red is a reprieve and a chance to be safe and proud with what he wants to read. In theory you honor and cherish the interests of the child, are you game for a little practice?

Get the book out of the pocket and onto the desk. Salve your conscience by complimenting him for removing the sexy cover. (By the way, he hasn't destroyed it. It graces the inside of his locker door.) Read the book yourself. It probably is "questionable," but what are the questions Red seeks to answer in its pages? Are its answers good enough for starters? Do you know of better ones that he will take as "better"? The three "dirty" words on page sixty-two are the monosyllables he hasn't misspelled in four years of literary efforts in latrine and corridor. You know what he's trying to find out. Can you help him to a healthy discovery?

But you know that S-E-X isn't the really big problem, despite its terrifying proportions. Red is trying to learn what his self is all about. He needs assurance that being a human being is important. He wants to know that he counts and why he counts. He is adolescent and desperately needs to be assured that he really is normal. And topping both of these needs, he has to have opportunities to try out for life roles. That's where the hotrods, the telescopes and the science fiction come in. And all of this adds up to a quest for a system of workable values that can make life worth the living. (That last sentence is a mistake. It's too grand. It is too pontifical. It sounds like the kind of statement written in college term papers for inspirational courses about the aims of education. The young teacher who survives in the profession learns quickly that there are more immediate and modest goals to be reached. Values, indeed! That is the job for home and church or perhaps the Boy Scout troop—*or is it?*)

That note never got into the teacher's mailbox. It remains in the invisible file where all the unwritten letters of protest and complaint are kept. And Red will probably grow up to say, "I haven't read a book since I left high school and if I live right, I never will!" He will get his answers somewhere else. They may be mass-produced slogans—the boiled down, predigested homilies by which many of us announce our acceptance and understanding of the world about us. They may be those unspoken, because unspeakable, "right feelings" about conduct and loyalties by which we guide so much of our behavior. In the long run, Red won't even remember that he was ever short-changed. He will never know that he is emotionally and morally smaller than he might have been. He might suspect that he is "smart enough" to have done as well, intellectually, as some of his better-book-fed schoolmates. But he will have learned to use little scorn-shaped tricks to make up for the apparent social distance between him and them.

Red will leave school, not as a non-reader; but he will have been successfully inoculated against all reading that is not plainly functional. He may even go to college, for he will have learned how to endure book-born suffering. He may even survive inescapable "literature" courses or their watered down "cultural" cousins, those supermarket survey courses that teach how to look without seeing at the historic, ethical and esthetic panorama of the human enterprise. With some kind of a diploma in hand attesting to the fact that he has "had it," he will turn to something that educators call the "world of work," free at last, from the tyranny of the book. He will join the huge majority of our population who never read anything if they don't have to.

Perhaps we should pause to consider whether all this ruckus about reading isn't after all a tempest in a discarded teapot. Can't we just say that some people find books important in their lives, for a variety of reasons and that a great many do not, and that this apparently has always been the case, and let it go at that? After all, it is quite evident that some of the functions of the book are now performed far more effectively and efficiently by radio and television. To be sure the educational aims of these media are embarrassingly modest and the intellectual stimulation provided by their best efforts has the crack-voiced callowness of a schoolboy. In spite of all the protests to the contrary, radio never quite "came of age" and there is abundant evidence that it is approaching senility. Although the movies are striving toward adulthood the burdens of maturity appear more than they can bear. How television will fare will depend upon its ability to educate its creative super-ego and control its commercial id. But however they develop, these mass media have easy entry into our homes. The wealth they offer may be tinsel, but it is dirt-cheap. Attention must be paid to a book, but they require no voluntary attention at all. The mass audience is passive, accepting emotional and intellectual handouts. The book has never been kind to beggars.

On the surface this statement is as unjust as it is inaccurate. The publishing industry is also in the entertainment business. Before the Audio-Visual Age, and now during it, publishers have fought for and captured large audiences of relatively passive consumers. The mass-circulation magazines have fallen heir to most of them, but most of them, too, are staring, open-eared at the front end of the tamed oscilloscope. The rest leaf through picture essays and comic books. The murder mystery and Western still make money for both writer and publisher. So will a tale of tarnished romance. As long as the book can explore human peccadilloes with more "honesty" and "freedom" than radio, film or television, there will be people to paw the pages of secret passion.

And yet *there is a danger in this kind of reasoning*. While it appears to proceed from a straightforward "description" of facts, it is actually selecting from the facts those that will separate the readers from the non-readers, to the detriment of the latter. It is a way of arguing that implies the existence of some sort of intellectual elite and that this elite gets that way from reading books. But as Joseph Warren Beach once said, "Critics are caught in semantic traps and the poets are sued for the damages." There is not *an* elite there are many. Each such group does achieve its status, in part, from the ability of its members to do certain kinds of reading efficiently. This is not saying anything very unusual or, in itself, very important. The guiding personalities in all professions gain their eminence through their ability to identify, select and use pertinent information. They are capable of taking pains to take the kind of thought that can and does lead to successful action. They are specialists in one field, but like all specialists, they are merely lay people in almost every other area of human endeavor. Thus a psychiatrist may have an intense amateur interest in archaeology, but among archaeologists, he merely sits in the audience and listens or reads. A labor leader may be widely sophisticated in those public matters that concern the welfare of his union but beyond the domain of his specific skills, he too, listens, as a lay person, to the specialist.

The requirements of modern technological society call for all sorts of highly specialized technical skills. In more and more of the professions there are fewer and fewer "all 'round men." The general practitioner is a museum piece, a storybook character, a luxury that can only be suffered in the underdeveloped corners of our economy. The specialist knows more and more about less and less. We can watch him learning in our schools and universities. How quickly the embryo professional has his nose pointed to a "specialty." It would seem almost, as if one of the last refuges of the generalizer is

to be found among elementary school teachers. Schools of education deserve some modest praise for their attempts, however unsuccessful, to bring the teacher's mind into a wider focus, in courses
in the humanities.

We have to fight against the disorganizing effects of too many
specialists and not enough generalizers. For as David Lilienthal has
said, ". . . the quality of unity in thinking has been displaced by
the philosophy of the specialist." [1] If this world is to have more
meaning for our children and their children, we have to grow up
to the ancient skill of generalizing upon the experiences of the times
in which we live. We may no longer be able to see life "steady"
as Socrates asked; there is too much motion today for that, but we
can see it "whole."

And this brings us again to the boy in the back of the room. He
may or may not be a candidate for membership in one of the elite
groups. That depends upon what kind of physical and psychological equipment he starts with. He must become a specialist if he is
to stay in our society. Even if he leaves it he will have to specialize
in withdrawal or escape. But whatever he becomes, however far he
develops, the kind of person he becomes will depend in a large
measure upon the quality of experiences he has now, in and out of
school; in and out of books. Even more important, it will depend
on the kinds and quality of responses he makes to these experiences.
Finally, it will depend upon the picture he has of himself.

There is a lot of talk, both theoretical and descriptive, among
psychologists about the tremendous need for the kind of educational program that will help children and young people generally,
get clear and realistic attitudes about "self-acceptance." There is controversy too, as to whether or not any teaching for self-acceptance
can do anything more than force the child to conform. But both
conformity and self-acceptance, at this level of discussion becomes
bewildering to the layman (who in this instance is everyone but
the psychologist).

Teachers, especially in the lower elementary grades have for a

---

[1] David Lilienthal, *This I Do Believe,* New York: Harper and Brothers, 1949, p. 55.

very long time been placing increasing emphasis upon the social development of the child. Although they tend to proceed by a sense of touch, they are not altogether amateurs in the field of child psychology. They have learned a great deal from men like Gesell and Terman and Jersild. They have been able to correlate social, psychological and physiological development of children with the general requirements that the community places upon the school. In the upper grades they run into trouble. The sense of touch, the almost instinctive insight that the teacher brings to the problems of teaching six-, eight- and ten-year-olds, seems to become less and less operative in dealing with the adolescent years, with results that are often unhappy for both teacher and child. When theory becomes too far separated from practice, both tend to go different ways and more time is spent talking about problems than in dealing with them.

Red is not alone as he might have appeared in the plaintive letter to the teacher. American school systems long ago moved beyond the primitive, three-R concept of education and have been providing both within the curriculum and at the administrative level a complex network of social and psychological services which are all directed toward helping the child and the parent to develop and experience the kinds of relationships that can go far toward assuring the growth of healthy attitudes as well as healthy bodies. As Jersild has said; "All children are more or less troubled; some of them are very much troubled." [2] He is not saying that they are maladjusted, a dangerous word. He is merely describing an important fact of child life. Why shouldn't they be troubled? At the age of five they move from the stable security of the family into the strange new world of the kindergarten. After a year in which they learn to live with a rather large group of children their own age, they move into classrooms that resemble the garden in many ways but are also radically different in some subtle ways. The business of learning is a little more formalized. There are unavoidable responsibilities to

[2] Arthur T. Jersild, *In Search of Self,* New York: Bureau of Publications, Teachers College, Columbia University, 1952, p. 5.

be accepted. Differences among the other children become apparent. He can see this especially in reading. Anxieties begin and in many cases he finds that his parents have been infected by these anxieties. Why shouldn't he be troubled?

He makes his "adjustments," his peace, with the changing routine and when he has reached the dizzy heights of the sixth grade with all its maturity and the grand status it gives him, he is dashed back into the mold of the little people once again. In junior high school, he is *only* a seventh grader. If there are no junior high schools in his community, he goes a little higher before he is tossed at the bottom of a huge high school hive, the lowliest of all creatures, a *freshman*. Added to these troubles, his body begins to play tricks on him. There are the pimples, his voice won't behave, his clothes don't fit very long, his muscles rebel, he trips, stumbles and bangs into things. And beside all this, it seems as if the whole adult world is in league against him. Of course he is troubled. So is his girl friend! Even more so. In the elementary school, teacher would say, "Hold hands!" and it was very natural to hold hands with the little girl next to you—but now, the high school teachers don't say that.

What's more, if you do, they frown, and say you shouldn't, in a very embarrassing way. And then there's the business of sex—and you discover that adults have such filthy minds! Of course you're troubled! And things can get so *boring!* The teachers drone on and on, for hours it seems, about the most ridiculous things. The funny business about nouns, and that algebra stuff—who needs algebra? And history, all those dead people! And science—it's silly where it isn't gruesome. And when you really get interested in something and you want to talk to the teacher, she's busy, or she's got a headache or she's got to hurry home.

Well, this teenage complaint is a long one. It has filled many novels and some mental hospitals too. But the schools have done much that was never done before. There are school people who are not in a hurry. The guides, or counselors, or home room teachers, whoever they are who have found the time to learn the skill to be usefully friendly. They listen and they help. Yet, is it any wonder that the adolescent views the help in this way:

Almost always they are on your side. They even help you get away from teachers who "hate" you. They don't laugh and they don't usually scold. They are almost always fair. They really help. But that's not enough. There are some things that it is very hard to talk about to adults or even to the other fellows. Mostly, you need a dark night under a street lamp, or a sleep-out with a friend where you can talk in bed in a darkened room, where you don't have to look at each other. That's when you can talk over the really big problems.

Talking to somebody else is sometimes very hard. It's better when you used to talk to yourself, but after a while you go round and round. Day-dreaming is good, but sometimes you get lost, and it's a bad habit because people are always watching, and when you do it in math class, you always get caught and it's very embarrassing. Books help—almost any kind of book, even comics. Animal stories are very good for some things, wild animals especially. You can really *be* that animal. Smart, tough, big-hearted—nothing is too hard for you. Like the lone wolf that crossed half a frozen continent in search of his mate—the fights he had, the way he got out of the forest fire—how he escaped the hunter's trap—how he took over a pack and became boss of the mountain range until he remembered the call, and dashed across the frozen wastes to find his mate again, just as the young ones were being born. Boy, if men could be as good, and simple and honest and reliable as that—if life could just be living. And then you figure—gee, if a smart animal could do this, you could really do it—because you can think, you can really plan. You can look ahead. You can learn.

Adults and even teachers get so bored with you when you read a lot of animal stories. They are in such a hurry for you to read stories with people in them and you can't explain that there are animal stories with people in them like in *Lassie Come Home* and the Island Stallion books and *The Yearling* even. What's good about those animal stories is the way one wonderful, terrific creature is a one-man (or one-girl) animal who falls in love with his young master and will do anything to stay with him. Those animals are a lot better than most of the people you meet, but it makes you feel good to see how they really depend on a fellow even if he is just a teenager.

The adolescent's quest for identity runs through all literature and all folk lore. He wants to make sure of the *I* that he is. The search is complicated if there are very many people in the story. Sometimes one is too many. He can identify with, and in fact become, the noble, savage animal. He is the very boy whom the dog loves and obeys. This is the way he gets visions of his own possible greatness. A boy's thoughts are long, long thoughts. They are delicately balanced between possibility and necessity. His success in this juggling will mark the way that he addresses himself to reality. Animal stories are helpful in this matter but they don't go far enough. They don't give enough scope. They don't provide the range of experience that human beings are capable of having, in the matter of finding out who you are and what you are worth. This is where the adventure story comes in. Man against the elements, man alone against the ravening forces of nature or pitted against inscrutable evil foemen. Nature is a blind opponent. There is a mountain to be climbed, a desert to cross, a shipwreck or plane crash to survive. Man alone, with courage and cunning, with desperate patience and fearful thought, works his way to ultimate, solitary victory. This is a way a boy can take the measure of man's possibilities. This is an index of potential greatness.

Stories about the battle against the evil doings of evil men gives a chance to try out the worth of the simple virtues that appear so plainly in the animal stories. In such tales good and evil directly confront each other. The bad guys are completely bad. They are silhouettes of the vices. The good guy is also plainly drawn, but he gets a little more substance since he is the one to be identified with. There are no shades of gray here. The characters are either for you or against you and hesitation in the alliance comes only from lack of forthcoming information. But there can only be one outcome. The moral and spiritual values win out in the end. Evil is unmasked and the future is bright and clean. Man can choose the right and the right is worth all the pains and sorrows it costs to gain.

The teenager has an insatiable appetite for any story that can give him further assurance of the power and worth of life as the human being can live it. He wants to be able to say "This can be me. This really *is* me!" He will go to any lengths to get this. Mythology, tall tales and folk lore, no matter how fantastic, how unreal, provide a rich source of such material. The ancient gods may be quaint and queer. The monsters, seen in the light of day, are cardboard threats and the world they people is no larger than the shadowy corners of the room. But when he enters that world through the pages of the book, he really is there. It is as big, as powerful as his own real world. He *is* Siegfried, Jason, Odysseus and Roland, and they are him. They are what he feels himself able to be—strong, courageous, intelligent, honest and even wise. The good that men do, they do for goodness' sake alone. Glory and fame are automatic. These heroes come to the teenager with the smile of the girl who would worship him, if she only knew. They come with the grudging respect he knows his father would give, if he only realized. They come with the love of his mother when she mixes it with pride in his accomplishments. In the world of myth, things are just this simple. The line between sunlight and shadow is sharp. The early adolescent cannot afford the luxury of a middle ground when he is learning how to identify his society's basic values.

Our first heroes are larger than life. Parents are almost god-images and our early teachers are kindly protective giants. The heroes in our story books have the same character, the same dimensions. The heroes of the myths, even if they are man-sized, have characteristics and capacities beyond the reach of mere men. But all these experiences of childhood and early adolescence prepare us to read the symbols of the valued personality and the useful action. When we turn to the record of human achievement in biographical writing, we are prepared to read these symbols with some accuracy even in the context of real, conflicting social actions. The life stories of real men and women, who once were children, who suffered and enjoyed the storms and stresses every teenager knows, allows the young reader to come to closer grips with the consequences of being a person, an individual.

Steinmetz had a brilliant mind in a twisted little body. He was capable of loving greatly. It was a long time before he found some people who were able to love him in return. Yet he was a giant, cut in the hero's mold, standing alone against the elemental lightnings, armed only with a pencil, a head full of mathematical formulas and a profound knowledge of the secrets of nature that are no secrets to science. Lindbergh was little more than a boy when he put tiny wings to a fierce dream and conquered the ocean air. Admiral Byrd lived alone under the snow near the South Pole and thought and wondered about himself and life and the meaning of both. When he was released after months of self-imprisonment, he was richer and wiser, as the Indian braves were after the fasting and the visions. A boy would learn much, reading Byrd's autobiographical report of this experience, entitled *Alone*.

When boys and girls can live for a while with the men and women who have made this world a different and often a better place, they may learn a little more about themselves. The horizons of early youth are always expanding. The whole world is a frontier. How does one live a life of adventure? How does one live on a frontier? The men and women in science, working alone and together, gambling the strength of their minds and the resources of their bodies and personalities against the unknown—the other kinds of world changers—the social reformers, the politicians, the engineers, the artists in every field—they all lived their lives in some ways out beyond the reach of their fellows on frontiers. They leave the records of the impact on their lives of the times in which they lived. The boy or girl who reads about them can be profoundly persuaded that life can be important, that it can be a grand and wondrous thing to be a member of such a race, that giants and heroes may be physically very ordinary people, wearing ordinary clothing. The part they played is open to all who come after them. This is what it means to be a human being.

This kind of reading, this kind of living-through the lives of others, be they animal, hero or man, helps the teenager gain self-assurance, helps him to come to terms with himself, to learn to like himself, to have confidence in the possibilities that are open to him because he is what he is and the world is what it is. But a healthy self-image is not enough.

The teenager wants to know himself as an individual, but he does not want to be so unique that anyone could notice the difference.

Notice how anxious he is to wear the same clothes as his friends, to have his hair cut the same way, to speak the same way, to be in the same class, go to the same school. He worries about being too tall, too short, too fat, too skinny. He is fascinated and terrified by any kind of abnormality. Diseases and wounds thrill and frighten him. He tries to face up to them by talking about them. He will turn to horror stories from any source, to inoculate himself with understanding, against these ever growing fears. He needs to learn that his individuality, which he prizes, is the sum of these very differences that now make him uncomfortable. But he can't be told.

His emotions and feelings raise psychological doubts that are even more acute and painful than his worries about physical differences. They whirl about in his mind with such force that he sometimes comes to doubt his own sanity. These are the dark dread secrets he can tell no one for no one ever felt the way he does about girls.

He has been learning all his life that sex is another spelling for sin and both mean filth. He has been lectured at about clean minds and healthy bodies. He has been warned that the penis is the key to the gate of hell. Everywhere he turns they point at him but he just can't seem to learn. He has terribly "sinful" habits. Even the words that name them are dirty. People only use them when they are angry or they want to hurt you. The other fellows say there are laws against it and you can get sick or even go crazy. So you joke and laugh the way they do, and you go home and worry.

Things are so mixed up. You look at your mother and father. Do they know? They try to talk to you and it's very embarrassing and everyone begins to argue. They don't like the kids you pal around with. Dating is all right with them if you go out with a nice girl, but their idea of a nice girl is boring. But you can't tell them because then they'll know. They tell you about working harder and paying more attention to schoolwork and just like the teachers they complain about daydreaming. Things are so mixed up. You like music, not just rock'n roll, but the sweet stuff and some of the classical music too. And you like poetry about death and beauty and every once in a while it looks as if painting can mean something too— But all this gets mixed up with sex somehow—how can you talk about that? If you talk about beauty to some of the fellows, they'll laugh at you and walk funny and call you queer. If you talk about the other stuff to your parents or the teacher— what can you do?

He's in a dilemma and sending him to books seems to be an awfully weak-kneed way of handling the situation. Some parents and some teachers are able to help him resolve the situation. Most are not. A good guidance counselor, with adequate psychological training could be very helpful. They are not found in many schools. But he needs to work this out by himself, as much as possible. Books it is, then—but not the "advice to young people" type that accentuates fears and gets rid of differences with sledge-hammer moralizing. Not the watered down books on personal adjustment with neat little stories about the neat little problems of clean-faced boys and girls in Hollywood-happy homes. What he needs is real people in real situations, three dimensional human beings with all the fears and limitations he has, and more. He'll find them too with a little help and no hindrance. If his reading experiences up to this time have been happy and successful, the problem is manageable; but if his reading skills are weak and poor, he will be cut off from this source of strength unless someone realizes the power of his need as a motivating force. He can make up his deficiencies in short order under appropriate guidance and compassionate instruction.

The teenager needs to be able to deal with his reactions, to test them out, to experiment with them so that he can find out whether what is happening to him is normal to human beings. It is something that is very hard to talk about. Not only is it embarrassing, it is intangible, it is not a problem like pimples or a changing voice. This is why he searches for stories about "someone just like me, a fellow going to this kind of school, who isn't good in sports and doesn't like girls." He can be very specific. In his hunger he could almost write the story. But he is looking for the assurance of the printed page. He wants to know that the same things that are happening to him, have happened before to someone else. He wants a book where there is a lot of digging into the way the characters feel and think about the kinds of problems that are now troubling him. This is why there are certain titles which remain popular for decades and even generations. Maugham's *Of Human Bondage* is one; Thomas Wolfe's *Look Homeward Angel* is another. They deal honestly and adequately with the inner turmoil, the roiling storms of youth. It is common experience among teachers and librarians that if such a book, really seems to be able to serve such purposes, it will be read eagerly even though it apparently is far beyond the reading level of the boy or girl. Books are good companions. They don't talk back, neither do they laugh. Secrets are safe with them.

The early adolescent's questions about his uniqueness and his differences, about his private status and his public membership in the human race are not settled easily or soon. They are added to by a third kind of question. "What am I to become?" He has been trying to answer that since he decided to be a fireman. But now he has a lot more to go on. He knows quite a bit about himself. He has talents and desires. He has thousands of hours in solo flight, daydreaming. His imagination has helped him be caveman, priest and king. In books and dreams and television reverie he has built empires, tamed the atom and won the girl with the laughing eyes. He has told great presidents what to do. He has died of everything from the Black Plague to the atom bomb. He has been hated by black-hearted enemies and loved by half the human race. But lately the roles he plays in the dreams he chooses have more reasonable demands. Military service is only a few years away. So is the cockpit of a jet plane. He has already tinkered with a hotrod. The designing engineer's drawing board is not so far away. He has been the star of the junior high school dramatics club. Broadway comes just after summer stock.

Some of these roles he may play, others he must. He has already learned that society will insist on the Army and on some kind of work. He knows that parenthood is a probability. He sees that citizenship is usually more than accidental. He already holds membership in several community groups either through the church, the Boy Scouts, the Police Athletic League or some other teenage group or gang. He has already learned much about living and working with others. Now he wants to know more. He may be a young man in a hurry, zeroing in on some life-work objective. He may be more than vaguely troubled because he has no clear idea about it. He may be able to defer it for a while through college plans, but not for very long. He has to have some clear idea or a group of related ideas about the things he would like to do, the things he is able to do and the things he will have to do as a member of society.

The school has always tried to help in this matter. In recent years it has put this help on a more professional basis, but vocational guidance is not enough. A list of requirements, a range of opportunities may be related to the capacities and talents of a boy or girl. It may help them to a realization of the possibility of success for them in a given field. It is all very interesting and helpful, but it is not enough. How does it feel to be a medical missionary? What does it feel like to be a toolmaker? What is the real life of a real secretary really like? Stories that are merely about such work are useful, but they are rarely written with answers to these questions in mind. The career books at the junior high school level tell what a job is about, but they barely touch the questions about why people choose such jobs and how they feel as they carry them out.

In asking these questions, the adolescent is looking for something that can be found most abundantly and honestly portrayed in the work of serious artists. The books or stories need not be great literature, but they must be honest attempts to see some aspect of life in ways that are meaningfully related to the hopes and plans and problems of real people. This of course, goes far beyond vocational guidance in one direction, the direction of feeling, while it hardly scratches the surface, in most cases, so far as the job or profession is concerned. Reading *Arrowsmith* gives a shadowy idea of what kind of study and planning goes into the making of a medical research scientist. Yet for the adolescent it can be a brilliantly clear portrait of a man who is such a doctor, struggling with his ideals against the corrosive effects of trying to get on in this world. It is social

criticism. It is an examination of values. It gives the reader a chance
to participate in Arrowsmith's experiences. It gives a chance to play
a role and in the playing to gain some understanding of what it is
like to defend and to lose and to protect some of the ideals that
make life worth living.

For the adolescent in this period reads to extend the range of his
human experience with more earnestness than ever before. Experience becomes, in fact, an end in itself. How does it feel to have
killed someone? He can live with Raskolnikov in *Crime and Pun-
ishment* and suffer, love, hate and lose and finally gain a soul-
shriving enlightenment. What is it like to die, to become a mother,
to be a thief, to live two thousand years ago as a Greek slave to a
Roman lecher? What is it like to be a saint or to laugh at the idea
of God? What is it like to see one's life work turn to ashes? For,
more than answering the questions "what may I become" and "what
is it like to be . . .", this kind of reading experience takes the adolescent to the very roots of human concern. It takes him, if he can
survive the journey, to the ultimate questions with which the mature
person must be prepared to live for the rest of his life. This kind of
reading is a part of the years-long confirmation ritual, out of which
he can emerge, truly a man.

This is not claiming or asking too much of reading or of the
reading child. This is not descriptive of some rising young intellectual or spiritual elite who will save us from whatever next assaults
our world or our ways of life. Happiness, peace of mind, productive
thinking (both negative and positive) are functions of and consequences of the behavior of human beings towards themselves and
each other. Whatever their political or religious persuasion people
cannot love what they do not understand. They cannot understand
what they cannot know. They cannot know what they have not
experienced. Human life isn't long enough or large enough for us
to learn very much any more. So we are dependent to a degree
never before felt, upon the artist, the professional thinker, and the
poet in both of them, to help us to organize and "forge out of the
smithy of my soul, the uncreated conscience of my race." It is be-

coming easier every year for us to become better, that is, more efficient specialists. It is not so easy for us to become better human beings. It is not too difficult to agree upon what we mean by "better"
but there is wide disagreement on how to become better.

There is a problem of desegration far more complicated than the
one some of us are now trying to solve in the schools and it is a
far older one; it too is in the schools.

Educational philosophers have for generations now, been urging
that we respect, celebrate and provide for the individual differences
we find in our children. They have been urging us to consider the
fact that intelligence can be and is expressed in other ways than
the mere manipulation of verbal symbols. The psychological sciences have in recent years been offering evidence in support of this
view. At times the teachers colleges have preached this almost as a
new dogma and have sent forth instructed disciples into the field.
But learning about these differences in a psychology course and dealing with them in a classroom is quite another matter. Even when
the teacher can recognize these differences, and sometimes they
are most subtle, it is no simple matter to exploit them for the benefit
of the individual in ways that are not costly to the class as a whole.

Good classroom teaching in secondary schools today at its best is
very exciting both for the teacher and the student. Some examples
of it can be found in most school systems, but not all and never
anywhere nearly enough. In theory there ought never to be any
"busywork." Everyone should be engaged in something that is both
interesting and meaningful. The purpose for which any instruction
or study is undertaken should always be clearly before the class.
The children should come together in groups according to their interests and their needs. The direction in which the class moves, in
its course of study, should be a function of the teacher's understanding of the needs of the children in subject matter and in intellectual and social skills, in combination with the class' understanding of those needs and the use of those skills.

No skill is ever learned unless it is put to use. So it is with reading. To think that this complex skill is being taught when the

child learns to reproduce the noises that are represented by marks on the printed page, is to miss the central point of democratic education. These noises, as we have seen many times, become words only as the child becomes able to assign accepted meanings to them. These meanings are appropriate and become useful when he can understand what the author is trying to say. This understanding becomes valuable when he can employ the ideas it contains in dealing with the daily experiences that confront him. With these ideas he must be able to organize and order those experiences in such ways that are productive of useful learnings.

The source of these experiences is the whole world about him in space and time. It is the pressure of all our yesterdays upon the affairs of today. It is sunspots and snowstorms. It is Arab and Israeli. It is election campaigns and the price of pork. It is the Junior Prom and a mother's careful lie. It is dead poets and coziness and irregular French verbs. It is the hunger of hate and the fullness of love and the faces you can't forget.

With all we know about growing up and all that we can't remember, the school and the teacher defend the child's right to free access to experience. Some experience is close at hand. The school is a social institution in a real community. With the teacher as a guide, a companion or sometimes merely as an interested observer, the children can learn much about effective ways of living together. Today in many schools the children plan with the teacher the courses of study they intend to embark upon. The exercise of citizenship rights and responsibilities begin in the early grades and blossom into full-fledged student governments in the secondary schools. As the child grows up more and more opportunities are available for him to learn to live and work with his fellows. This is fine, but it is never enough. It never has been enough. That is why the reading life of the child needs such enrichment. To reach beyond the classroom, beyond the town into the world of people, into their minds, the book and the story are still the sovereign instruments.

As we have already seen, the family must prepare the child to discover the need and the value of reading. It must begin by according to the act of reading a status at least equal to the viewing of television. A reading family is the best assurance against a reading failure. An appetite for reading has to be acquired, as all but our most basic biological appetites must be. It is best if it is gotten early, but any adult is capable, with a little discipline, of providing the atmosphere in which the child can find reading pleasurable.

The school's job, at the beginning, is relatively easy. It almost seems mechanical, although it never is. From the very beginning, as the fundamental skills are mastered, the child must get out of his reading more than he puts into it. His interests must be honored. He must be entertained. Instruction must be supplementary to his widening needs for new experiences. The story must literally *tell* him something about himself. In the relatively secure years of childhood this something is not very much; throughout adolescence it is a great deal. The book that we choose to put before him, whether we are parents or teacher, must be considered in terms of what it can show about the value of human life; what it can demonstrate about our ability to master the situations that confront us. What does it say about loyalties? How can he discover the nature of responsibility to ideas, ideals, and to his fellows? In what ways does it portray the growth of character? Is it a fair representation of the relations between failure and victory? To what extent does it exercise his thought and his emotions? These questions imply, of course, that we should read the book, or at least enough of it, to know what might happen, when he reads it.

Although we as adults are concerned to give the boy or girl the best possible reading experience, we cannot afford to overlook the fact that he has learned to make reading choices on his own. We ignore these choices more than we honor them. And tolerance is not enough. Don't forget the hungers that send him to these books. Don't be so quick to depreciate the shoddy magazine, the blatant paperback, even the ghastly comic. You can easily see what he is after. Find out if he is getting it. Honor his struggle and help him on to the kind of reading that will feed his hunger with stronger food. A wise, courageous and patient adult, teacher or parent, who is willing to help him on to better reading, will begin by accepting the teenager where he is. What he is reading is of vital importance to him, however trivial it seems to us. Too often the teacher rejects the very material upon which a vital reading program must be based. You cannot begin with the "classics," with "rich" and "ennobling masterpieces." If they are that, and much of the so-called literature that we parade before our youth most certainly is not, if they are that, then they provide secret goals toward which you can strive. The children are often more realistic in this matter than we are. An eighth-grade girl said to her teacher, after having seen several telecasts of some plays, "Gee, I can't wait until I learn to read well enough to read Shakespeare!" This is no cue for the teacher to rush to the library for an appropriately "edited" text. The girl is wise in her reluctant patience. A little help with the diction, a little direction with the story line, some carefully planned selections read well, by someone who knows how to read aloud—such an approach may help, but most of all patience.

When we set out to talk about books with the adolescent, we should be very cautious about following the "discussion guides" that abound in the modern high-school textbooks. In adult discussions, unless we are very sophisticated about such matters, we rarely begin by talking about such matters as the "writer's craft," the delineation of character, the structure of plot. Why should we then direct the student's attention to them? Let us begin rather with the recognition that something happens *to* anyone who reads anything. Let's talk about that. We know some of the things the students are after. What makes a man or a woman behave the way the central character does? What was the boy who informed on his friends trying to show? Why is it that you really like the villain so often? How can people bring themselves to do such awful things? How do you find the strength to suffer so much for a principle and what are principles anyway? Has anything like what you read about ever happened to you? How did you act? Are you willing to talk about that? Why or why not?

After questions of this kind directed to the central interests of the reader, then it is possible and occasionally even desirable to go on to an examination of other aspects of the reading experience. The qualities of the literary experience have wide and profound ramifications. They are rooted in the quick and close aspects of daily life and they extend through the psychological areas in to the esthetic. You may begin by catching "beauty unawares," but to talk about it takes some doing, some living. How is it that there can be beauty in a story of anger and hate? How is it that you can feel good after reading about tragedy? How is it that a happy ending can leave you feeling cheated? How is it that an author can speak of the grandest things on earth by using simple little words to describe very ordinary happenings?

The reading experience of any of us, most especially the children, deserves opportunities for honest responses. Such responses are frustrated if we are catechized about plot, style and story line. It is of little significance if we can remember who did what to whom or when the author was born, or what a critic said he thought the author said, unless we also know something about what happened to us as we read and have some idea why it happened.

In this discussion we have been concerned mainly with the reading of fiction but what has been said here about interests, needs, and responses applies as well to a mathematical formula, a scientific statement, a philosophical proposition, a historical report. Things happen to us because we read, and we read further because of what happens. This is what learning is, among other things. This is part of living too. To get at the meanings, to go behind the appearances of things, to find out the hiding place of the elusive "why"; these things we need to manage ourselves and the world in which we live.

In one way or another we are always faced with the problem of being ready to read. The six-year-old has to show "readiness" before he can begin to be taught the meanings of the basic symbols of the alphabet. The older student in college as well as in the secondary schools, is often assumed to be constantly "at the ready" for each new kind of reading experience. He very often is not. The young child can be readily shown that the word and the thing are different. The older child and the youth are sometimes easily persuaded by their mere verbal facility that the word exercises they engage in in recitation is the equivalent to understanding. Meaning is more than that. No matter how skilled we become in "remembering" what is written down, we haven't learned to read until we are able to relate the understanding we get out of this reading to the life we are living. Merely to be able to substitute one set of words for another is no evidence of this understanding. We must be able to tie into our own actual experiences the ones we get from the printed page and measure both against our widened understanding and our hopes.

11

Who Says I Can't Read?

Many earnest and confused critics of our schools will not be satisfied with the preceding chapter. We can hear them say: "Now let's be practical. Kids are getting into high schools and sometimes lasting through to graduation although they are almost illiterate. Children are promoted to higher classes when they grow out of the lower ones—physically, that is—and except in the most extreme cases this happens every year. In many of the classrooms where the majority of the students are unable to read the teacher doesn't even try to teach. She becomes a glorified and very expensive baby-sitter. This is a result of our archaic child-labor laws."

Let us follow this argument logically but without heat. The statistics of high school drop-outs show that, while most non-readers do quit before graduation, some do not. Some high school drop-outs, and they form an alarmingly large percentage, are among the fair and good readers. A majority of poor readers who do drop out of school actually have the mental capacity to read above the sixth grade level, yet almost none ever achieve this. What is really disturbing is that good and poor readers alike suffer from little or no help in reading instruction in the secondary schools. Many successful high school graduates, including those who go on to college, report that they feel that they could have greatly profited if they had had some kind of help in the improvement of reading skills. They didn't get it. They were short-changed.

If a boy or girl is to survive in high school, reading skill is essential. No matter what else the school claims or tries to do, if it is to perform its educative function, it must make efficient readers out of its students. No amount of social adjustment, no amount of sympathetic counseling or understanding can compensate the child for this lack. No one in our society achieves much without this fundamental skill. Something has to be done about it.

The first and most obvious thing to do is to fix the blame. Any instructor of college English will tell you how deplorably ill-equipped for college high school graduates are. Any high school English teacher, or the teachers in any of the subjects will tell how the junior high school teachers shirked their responsibility. They in turn will report with terrible accuracy the defection of the elementary schools. The upper grade teacher will wonder what the primary grade teacher does with her time. There's the culprit! Can she blame the kindergarten teacher or the nursery school? She is *it,* or is she? The children were all right, she will report. Look at the record. She mentioned the differences in readiness, noted the kinds of attention the child required, when she sent him on to the next grade. What did that teacher do? Well, the record shows that teacher also was aware of the differences in rate of growth and even pointed out the need for special assistance in several instances. There are the reports of parent conferences. The upper primary teachers separated the fast from the slow and called in the reading specialist at the right time —what has the reading specialist to say? Her records are clear. She administered the necessary diagnostic tests, did the corrective teaching and made the appropriate referrals to the psychologist and the guidance counselor for the cases that were beyond her competence. Her records show considerable success with most of the children who come to her with reading difficulties. She joins with the primary teachers in asking whether the upper grade teachers paid any attention to the recorded suggestions. So we have a circle of complaint.

Many of the children who enter secondary school with reading problems have long histories and long experience with failure in reading. Many who apparently might have been saved, if the resources of school and family had been great enough and had been properly employed, seem never to have had any attention at all. They were "written off." The plaintive statements of high school students, both graduates and drop-outs, attest to the fact that they never got any real help in reading.

The blame won't stay fixed! It is tempting to lay about us with the finger of scorn, but it is futile too. There is some satisfaction to be gotten in ripping the sense of statistics from the bleeding context of educational reports, but this only serves to demonstrate our blind and ignorant anger. The opening paragraphs of this chapter are written in the language of that ignorant anger. Ignorance is an invitation to learning only if it is not rejected in favor of the cheap receipts of prejudice.

Let us look at some stubborn facts again. In 1889 only 7 per cent of American youth of high school age were enrolled in high schools. In 1950 77 per cent were enrolled. In 1870 only 4 per cent of the young people in this country graduated from high school. Today more than 59 per cent graduate. Impressive as these figures are, they are tempered by the further statistic that even today less than 60 per cent of our children are getting a high school education.[1] The main reason for this continuing increase in high school enrollment stems from the conviction shared by professional educators and the public that every child should be educated to his intellectual capacity. There is however a persistent confusion about what education is. Most people still conceive of it as the acquisition of the three-R skills and as much information as can be gotten with these skills. The public still tends to measure the performance of our schools largely in terms of these acquisitions. Anything else that the school does is, despite all educational propaganda to the contrary, labeled as "frills," window dressing and play. An amazingly large number of teachers, both in their actions and in their behavior, demonstrate that they share these views. However sophisticated our educational policies and philosophies may be, majority opinion still sees the school as a Latin Academy, whose goal was "to give them their

[1] U.S. Office of Education, *Biennial Survey of Education in the United States,* 1948–1950, Washington, D.C., U.S. Government Printing Office, 1953, p. 15.

letters and make them into ladies and gentlemen." The printed word is still treated as a magic and learning means the command of letters.

Education begins with communication. Language is the most subtle, the strongest, and most extensive means we have of keeping in touch with the world about us. That is why language and the arts related to it get so great a reputation. But communication is more than words. Communication is the announcement of the existence of things and the doing of things. Education is the means by which we learn how to deal with our contacts with the world of thoughts, things and feelings. John Dewey said that, "What nutrition and reproduction are to physiological life, education is to social life." It is through education, both formal and informal, that we guarantee the continued existence of our society. It is through education that we feed back into our society the ideas and behavior patterns of individuals and groups that make our society as good as it ever was and makes provisions for its improvement.

Education is everything from manners to world management. It is training in tool-using, in bowel and bladder control, in accepting the do-and-don't laws that insulate us from and relate us to the world of things and people. In its simplest dictionary sense, the word education means just the process of leading or bringing up. This is the *tending* part of education with which the family is or should be concerned. But as life becomes more and more complicated, the family turns to the school for help. Since memory cannot be inherited, parents cannot recall what their parents asked the school to do for the child. As a result, they sometimes wonder at all the "other things" that the school tries to do for the child beside giving him the three Rs. This wonder is excited and exploited by those critics of education who seem to be more interested in making headlines than in making headway in the problems that the schools face. Fortunately most criticism is of a practical and responsible nature that is healthy and health-giving. Some of it is not, even though it might have been originally so intended. The more popularized criticism of reading programs and practice suffers from this disability.

The teaching of reading is not perfect. It cannot be in a changing world with a changing language. It is better than it has been in the past. This statement can be verified by anyone who is willing to spend a little time looking at the statistical records and the scientific data and observing the actual teaching of reading in enough classrooms to warrant useful generalizations about the practice. Not all teaching of reading is excellent. Some of it, especially in the higher primary grades and in the secondary schools is not anywhere nearly as good as it can be. Some children have great difficulty in learning how to read and a few perhaps will never be able to master the skill. But as has been noted repeatedly throughout this book, the presence of these failures is an index of the scope of the job we want the schools to do.

The reading of the printed page is today a different kind of task from what it was half a century ago. Then there were no competing agencies of information and few other sources for recreation. The desire and the need for learning how to read was acutely presented even to a very young child. Books were very much the furniture of the minds and homes of almost every member of society except for the illiterate base, and even there, the value of reading as a source of power and freedom was accepted. Public education had still a compelling newness, and especially for the immigrant, it was a jewel beyond price. The free library was in fact a powerhouse of knowledge most especially in the dark urban areas. It was in this atmosphere that reading acquired the reputation it still has.

Today's child, and adult too, uses reading far more selectively. There are certain functions that radio, the film and television perform with greater skill and economy than the printed page can, and we have learned to employ them well. As media for sheer entertainment they are unexcelled. As sources for quick information and news, they are unsurpassed by any form of learning, they are eminently useful.

Audio-visual teaching aids are wonderful devices to have in the classroom and in the home too. Television and the film can provide experiences of great and lasting value—but only on the printed page do we achieve that form of close and persistent communion between a learning and an informing mind—only with the printed page can the reader control the speed of information flow—only the printed page can hold ideas still long enough for them to be assimilated into the mind of the learning child. And yet . . .

The peaceful co-existence of print, sound and vision is to a large extent guaranteed by the psycho-physiological make-up of the human race. The basic division into visual, auditory and motorial types means that the primary and the strongest impulses are conveyed through the eyes, the ears and the muscles respectively. These types, though of course not clear-cut, are sufficiently differentiated to ensure the permanence, side by side, of three groups of people who derive the deepest impression and the greatest satisfaction from either reading words printed or listening to words spoken, or watching words acted.[2]

The limitations of these media are to a considerable degree the limitations of the minds that direct them. Further, the school has an additional assignment that it hasn't yet fully accepted. It will have to teach the child how to listen and look. If it does not, the child will grow into the kind of adult, that far too many of us are. Passive consumption of the material on loudspeaker and screen characterizes the most general use of these media. We look and listen, involuntarily, uncritically. Our responses to these experiences cover a very narrow range of feeling and thought. In short, the school will have to teach us how to "read" television, the film and radio. It has never done this adequately. Language and symbol in these media can have a rich and powerful capacity to help us to know ourselves and our world. We are in the midst of an esthetic revolution. We have new kinds of mirrors to hold up to nature. How clearly they reflect and how well we see will depend on how we are taught and how we learn to interpret what the waves and electrons write.

In the beginning of this book reading was described as a pervasive and complex activity which man commonly engages in as he deals with the world about him and within himself. It was suggested that

[2] S. H. Steinberg, *Five Hundred Years of Printing*, London: Penguin Books, 1955, p. 260.

the human being needs to be able to read in order to interpret correctly the features of this world, if he is to be able to identify differences among things. This success is a necessary prerequisite to the specific, specialized kind of reading that involves symbols printed or written on a page.

While these statements are deceptively profound, they actually describe very commonplace facts of human growth and development. The success we achieve in any kind of reading is first of all dependent on the basic physical and psychological equipment that we have. Some people are more intelligent than others. Some can see more clearly. Some can fix their attention on details for a long time. Some tire easily. People are different. They perform similar tasks with different degrees of efficiency. What we learn and how we learn it, is finally tested in the way we can use the knowledge we get. In civilized countries we try not to grade people according to size, shape and color. We try not to discount people because of family tree or birthplace. We try to act as if people are merely different, not better or poorer. We do not often succeed, and never as much as we would like, but we do try. Destructive criticism of a child's educational capacity or achievement is certainly one of our failures.

All children who are even moderately healthy manage to get about in this world and function as we expect human beings to do, most of the time. When they behave like animals or angels we are disturbed. When they are too "good" we have cause for worry. When they are too "bad" for too long a time, we are concerned. So long as this concern is modulated by love, they will survive and grow into useful and relatively happy adulthood. But love is apparently an elusive quality that gets mixed up with anxieties and our own adult eagerness for approval and for status. We like to be thought of as good parents of happy children and if it is necessary, we are sometimes willing to beat the little savages into accepting their roles in this scheme of things.

Still we worry, and this worry is readily exploited and turned into cash. The half-informed, semi-educated critic of contemporary education sees some of these children who have difficulty with reading and the few who cannot read at all and shouts in print that almost none can read. Taking one child and subjecting him to a rigorous program of training the critic gets results and ascribes his success to the almost exclusive application of phonic analysis. Usually he misunderstands his own program, for if his goal is to have the child do more than merely sound out the words, he will have had to employ most of the techniques that competent teachers of reading have been employing in the schools for many years. But complexity has low sales value, or so he thinks. The simple, clear, single cause is more readily grasped, more easily accepted. The all-in-one remedy can be attractively packaged and the parents are freed from any guilt or responsibility.

Teachers, timid souls that they are, are easily stampeded by the loud financial and popular success of their critics and they almost invariably respond by publicizing their detractors. Their behavior during recent years is typical. Conferences and conventions on the Reading Problem have been over-subscribed and attended. Where nine hundred teachers were expected, three thousand came. The guest speakers and discussion leaders made brave noises and considerable capital for themselves and the critic. Had the energy expended been directed toward the improvement of the reading programs in their own schools the result would have been far more than fixing the offending book for so many weeks so high on the best seller list. Some publishers, quick to see a ready-made market scraped together new books and re-issued old texts offering phonics in massive doses to both pupil and teacher. As the passion and the sales subside, the schools that have allowed themselves to be bilked into accepting these nostrums, are finding their old inadequate reading programs further crippled and their storeroom shelves overloaded with material designed to bore the children into submission.

Along with the critics of the mechanics of reading and in fact absolutely contradicting them, are the groups that indict the school for allowing the child to read the "wrong" things. There are quite a few road shows that have been traveling back and forth across the country for some years now, warning every village and town that our children are wallowing in "sex, filth and sin." They equate children's reading habits with the rise in juvenile delinquency. They correlate it with the rise, more fancied than real, of sex offenses. They attribute this "moral and spiritual degeneration" to the sale of comic books. They accuse publishers in general, not only publishers of the comics, of corrupting our youth and the remedy they have to offer is a combination of book-burning and the flouting of the constitutional processes. Their complaint can be met, they say, if we take this trash from the children's hands and give them a literary treasure. Their conception of treasure would make most children flee to the protection of the friendly television screen.

These people are never very well read; if they were, they would not be able to stomach their own behavior. Whenever they speak they demonstrate their abysmal ignorance of the mind and habits of the child and often, the very books and magazines that they offer as "treasure" are used by children in some strange and, to them, unhealthy ways. There is a national magazine that has been popular in schools for more than half a century. It generally has the approval of these road shows. This magazine has furnished many generations of school children with sexually exciting views of naked human bodies. This magazine has never hurt any child but the self-appointed guardians of public morals would rip it from the libraries if they only knew its contents. It is *National Geographic*!

There are other more legitimate critics of children's reading habits and skills. They are in a very ancient tradition. They object that boys and girls do not read as much or as well as they might because what they are given to read is so weak and stupid. They made this complaint in Babylon, in Athens, in Rome. They made it throughout the nineteenth century. They made it in the twenties, they are making it today. And they are always right.

When the adult writes for the child, he almost always aims too low. This, in itself, is not an unwise practice. The child is usually free and able to reach beyond the limits of any one writer. But one result is that at all levels of child interest there is an accumulating rubbish heap of unreadable stuff. For example; it is very important, as the child is getting his first sight vocabulary, to use simple words and to repeat them in as many different ways as the ingenuity of the author can devise. But a young man or woman of six years is profoundly shocked by such deathless prose as, "Look, Jane, look. See Jack hit the ball. Look at the ball." At first shock it is funny. Very soon it becomes a terrible bore.

Some of this kind of writing appears to be unavoidable until the child's reading vocabulary is brought closer to his everyday speaking vocabulary. It takes a long time to close the gap but there should be no excuse for the watered down, eviscerated prose that disgraces so many of the books that children and adolescents are given to read. And yet this criticism is mainly an index of the degree to which we extend our goals. Toward the end of the last century, books and magazines that were available to young people made very little effort to reach "down" to their interest level. *Youth's Companion* and *Saint Nicholas* magazines opened their pages to the finest writing talent in the English language. The authors addressed themselves to whatever interested them. They measured their success in terms of their ability to interest others, regardless of age or educational differences. As a result, many children who might have profited by reading such magazines, never got to them. Horatio Alger provided the story for these children. He rewrote it more than a hundred times under changing titles. His subject was always the same; the reward of virtue and hard work is material success; the sky is the limit and you can reach it. The theme is exciting. The poor boy who is honest is the one who makes good.

We smile at Alger's simple heroes but—as Wilson Follett wrote in the now extinct magazine, *The Bookman*:

This oft-told tale of adventure had at least the solid merit of being adventurous. Its suspense was contrived out of such threats as disgrace and stark indigence. Its triumph, however little "true to life", was a triumph over enemies that are powerful, disastrous and real, in life as well as in fiction. There was, in fine, something at stake worth writing a story about. Very different are today's tales of adventure for the young.

ЖЖЖЖЖЖЖЖ

They are written about the long and short vacations of Boy Scouts. No more does a solitary young man here struggle in the dark against malignant oppressions. Rather, a gregarious motley of youngsters—a fat boy, a tall, acrobatic boy, an absent-minded boy, an Irish boy with a comic supplement brogue, a camera fiend, and a wise all-around boy on whom the others lean for advice and everything else—go on chattering forays into the Rocky Mountains and the Maine woods and the Florida bayous. A two-pound bass is good for a long chapter; the plight of two lads night-bound in the woods five miles from camp is worth five chapters—six, if the two have no matches along. The most that can ever possibly happen is the boy's accidental discovery of the hide-out of some bank robbers; and the most that can come of this is their collection of a reward which finances another expedition—that is to say, commits the author to another book . . . .

It is impossible to resist the conclusion that such woefully written stuff, distributed by hundreds of thousands of copies a year to boys young enough to accept it as good, has a great deal to do, and will have more, with our national insensitiveness to the decencies of language, our frequent confusion of mere cheapness with humor, and our adult hospitality to printed matter equally defiant of all civilized standards.[3]

Only the date of this statement is surprising. Follett wrote this in 1929! The books singled out for this snarl are known to all of us who are over forty; *The Rover Boys, The Outdoor Chums, The Motor Boat Boys, The Putnam Hall Cadets, Tom Swift, Ted Marsh, Dick Hamilton, The Boy Allies, The Boys of Columbia High.* They were, as Follett says, pretty ghastly stuff. That we survived them at all, those of us who did, is a measure of the toughness of the human mind and the presence of other more challenging interests. Or is it? With very little editing, Follett's article could be republished today and every comment he made would still be pertinent. The formula story is still with us. The tiny, unimportant challenges still festoon the plot. The characters are still two-dimensional. But, just how much have we adults suffered from our own exposure to the pap of the past?

Despite all the dark pronouncements the children are still reading today. They are reading as well as we ever did. More of them are

[3] Wilson Follett, "Junior Model," *The Bookman,* Vol. LXX, Sept. 1929, O. 11.

better readers than we ever were. We are conscious of those who have difficulties. We are concerned about them and we try to help them. We often succeed.

Let us look at the teenager again. His day is fuller than ours was at his age. He doesn't have the protection of a forty-hour week. His is closer to eighty. In fact he hasn't yet discovered the values or virtues of leisure. School and homework take upwards of forty hours. Transportation can consume another ten. Family duties can take from ten to twenty hours. What is left he has to divide among sports, television, movies, girls, gangs, hobbies and day-dreaming. And still he reads more than most parents who complain louder but loaf longer than he does. Most of his own reading he does, as we have noticed, in spite of rather than because of the urging of the teachers and other interested adults. Some of his reading he has to carry on in hidden places, as thousands of generations of teenagers have always done. Yet this is good reading, highly efficient reading, far better in most ways than anything he does from 8:30 A.M. to 3 P.M. in school. He is reading for all of the many reasons we discussed in the preceding chapter. But there is no place on the report card for that kind of reading. There is no classroom test he can take or is given to measure the growth of his skill and discernment. No record is kept, outside of his own mind, of his adventures in reading, unless he chooses to keep it himself.

A good teacher is aware of the reading that her students are doing but she is rarely able to capitalize upon it. There are so many re- ctions, so much to be done. In many cases there is the tyranny lesson plan. Sometimes, often in fact, the shadow of the boards examinations and entrance requirements is present, ose who have no college plans. A few of these children o talk with even fewer teachers about their extra- sts, but for the most part they are strictly on their ue to read avidly and omnivorously up to the school. They read more during their middle ill again in their whole lives. Most of them they graduate because they have learned to read for the single narrow purpose of getting on, of passing grades, of getting specific information. The joy is wrung out of reading for them. Who does it?

Here is a challenge that Follett posed thirty years ago. If teachers or parents would only look at what it is we demand of our children in the way of reading and what we give to them to read, both in school and out, and if they would test the quality of this stuff against the known needs and requirements of our rapidly maturing citizens they would see that "the preposterous quality of what most of us hand to our youngsters (is, and) the resultant outcry would be a marvelously good omen for American (youth), American education in language—even, ultimately, for American publishing and printing." [4] It is here that the teachers, the parents and the school are most delinquent. The apparatus is available, the techniques are there. Enough good reading material is at hand for a start. But to date we have little more than muscle flexing and promises to get to work and "show them."

The elements are all present to meet this challenge today. There is an "outcry" by anxious parents, earnest educators, and critics, both passionate and commercial. There is a substantial and viable body of knowledge and techniques dealing with the subject of reading at all levels and conditions. There is the continually extending interest in the cultural as well as the practical values of reading. Basic literacy in the United States is now above 95.5 per cent. Librarians report that television, radio and the film, stimulate rather than retard reading, and they are supported by impressive statistics from many sources. Finally, there is a growing awareness, especially in the secondary schools, and to an unfortunately lesser extent in the colleges, of the need for the continued teaching of specific reading skill beyond the achievement of sixth grade competence. What has be clearly enough realized is perhaps the greatest of all these resou in meeting this challenge. The children are reading, and they l their reading careers by enjoying the act of reading.

A single program to meet this challenge is neither practi

[4] *Ibid.,* p. 14.

sirable nor, in the long run, even possible. A simple creed, a philosophy, an attitude towards the nature and uses of reading can be spelled out. It is already implicit in most of the painstaking scientific study and experimentation that is carried on in the schools and the clinics. It pervades the editorial policies of the best of the textbook publishers. It is continually being developed by professional teachers' organizations such as the National Council for Teachers of English, both in matters of material and methods of practice. Unfortunately not enough working teachers are aware of this and only a few parents have any knowledge of its existence.

Perhaps the parents can get things going. They should be encouraged to do so. It is not enough to hold membership in the P.T.A. or even to be a vocal committee worker. Parents are teachers in the first instance and reading must begin in the home. Your own home is the most important place, but you can't overlook your neighbor's, and the other places where your child lives and spends time. Although reading is eminently personal and ultimately individual, it has a community aspect that all experiences that are in any way capable of being shared must have. Books and other reading material must be widely available throughout the whole community. This means that there must be more and more easily accessible library services both of a public and a private nature. This means too, that book selling needs to be encouraged in the community. Look around you. How many places are there, within a fifty-mile radius where books are sold? Look at the school. Does it offer books for sale?

Yes, parents can start things. It is the considered judgment and the announced policy of most of the teachers' professional organizations that all teachers, regardless of what they teach or where they teach, be they gym teachers, shop teachers or even principals, are teachers of reading. Consider them for a moment. How many of the educators who are in contact with children are *readers* in the full and adult meaning of the title? How many of them not only do read widely but obviously do enjoy and are capable of communicating this joy in reading? The obvious answer, even before a search is made, is that far too few do. But only the pure may throw stones and they are too mature to do so. Teaching has become, for too many teachers so much of a chore, so much of a clawing, undignified scramble for subsistence, that they have little time for the amenities that reading requires. Teachers have to be helped to lead fuller lives if they are to be richer persons, able to give as much of themselves as they must give if they are to help our children become good people. Their problems cannot be simply solved by an ever-expanding paycheck.

All teachers have to be concerned about the reading habits of their students and not merely as complainers and buck passers. While it is true that the English teacher should be especially concerned with helping her pupils gain and extend their competence in reading in all areas, her function ought properly to be that of a liaison person who connects what every other teacher does to what every child needs to know. She should have at her finger tips the titles of thousands of books that boys and girls in the age groups she works with, can and will enjoy and find useful.

Unfortunately, most English teachers are considered extraordinarily fine teachers if their repertoire encompasses a few dozen titles. This poverty is absolutely unnecessary. In almost any school library or English department office, there are available dozens, and perhaps even hundreds of standard lists of books. Many of them are extensively annotated, so that the overworked teacher can even escape reading them herself. Where such lists have been lost or are hard to find, five minutes research and a few pennies in an envelope will bring them to her. Professional magazines like the *English Journal* are constantly reviewing children's literature and offering extended discussions of ways in which its reading can be encouraged. The book review supplements of most of the larger newspapers all carry reviews and notes of reading for the youngsters. No, there is no dearth of material. Its use is lacking because of overwork and under-enterprise on the part of the teacher.

But more reading material is never the sole answer. Parents should visit the classroom, talk with the children, see how reading is actually being taught. They will usually be impressed by the practice in the lower grades. But if they have become at all aware of the problem, they may be appalled at what passes for reading in the higher grades and in secondary schools. The same few tired old titles that bored them a generation ago persist. There are a few new candidates for oblivion added each year. Our literary "heritage" is chopped into assignment-sized morsels and parceled out over weeks of agony. If the teacher has any pretenses to modernity, she may have added a few fillips of "project" busywork such as posters, pantomime and models of pirate ships and guillotines. But *Silas Marner* will still be "analyzed" and Charles Darney will be "explored" and Shakespeare will be "done" to a turn. Class discussion, where it is entertained at all will be geared to some mystical least common denominator or prearranged textbook questions and what happens to the individual child because of what he has read will almost never be explored. It is small wonder in such an atmosphere that the boy or girl separates what goes on in the classroom under the banner of "reading" from what goes on between him and his books and his friends who have also read them and gotten joy, fear and information from them.

What is being referred to here is not the worst kind of teaching, in fact it might even have its own peculiar excellences. It is the kind of teaching that is all too common, all too general. It has a "job" aspect to it, an onerous requiredness about it. It is pedestrianism. It is earth-bound in an uncomplimentary way. It is morally tiny. It is meek. It is mean.

There are very few places in the modern school that are deliberately designed for the students to read in. A few enterprising schools have furnished small lounges which smack neither of the library nor of the classroom where a reader may learn how to suspend time and master space for a little while, but even here, the omnipresent bell will warn him on the quarter hour that school still keeps. Back he goes to the classroom where reading is shackled study or to the library with its tense hushedness, where things are "looked up" or magazine pages are the softly flipped flags of boredom.

Perhaps there is no help for such conditions in a big school in a teeming city. But elsewhere there should be time and space. The home is the logical refuge. The child's own room can be a vehicle, a kind of space ship, a veritable time machine powered by shelves of books and a reading mind. If the family has done its job, as teacher-in-the-first-instance, the child's room can easily make up for most of the lacks of any school. More than that, it can help the school to do some of the things that teachers dream about but so seldom have either the single courage or sufficient time to try.

So often teachers complain about the "quality of the boys and girls we are getting today" as though there were an absolute degeneration of the race. Children are certainly not as "tractable" as in other generations. They are more knowledgeable, they have wider interests, their experiences with ideas and things are greater than ours ever were. They are not ready, without a fight, to accept the notion that some of the things that are required of them in the school are as valuable as the school seems to think. Yet in this questioning attitude the school can find a source of power that can literally dissipate most of the so-called reading problems that plague it.

Regardless of the pious preachments of most educators we do not begin to respect the interests of children enough. Wherever their interests clash with the announced purposes of the curriculum, we demand that they knuckle under. We label as trivial, vulgar or worse most of the things they read for themselves. The teacher's defense, that she has to protect "standards" is often as specious as it is uninformed. (And we are still talking about the English teacher.) Her occasional retreat behind the skirts of public morality is unkind and cowardly. She often projects her own personality insecurities onto the girl or boy when she is faced by any of the apparently controversial areas of their interest. These include religion, sex, social practice, art, politics and science, in fact almost the whole gamut of human enterprise. She has usually terminated her own sentimental adventure with the world and living and becomes either fearful or romantically incompetent in dealing with the anticipated voyages of youth. She may not be very much older than her charges, but then, teachers age very quickly.

Teachers and administrators have for years been declaring that it is their responsibility and their aim to take the child where they find him, but in practice they shove him into a jungle-gym of required achievements before they even assess his actual position and condition. It can be claimed with considerable honesty that this is a matter of efficiency, that a teacher has just so much time, just so much energy, that she cannot split herself up into many persons. On the other hand, this would seem to deny or at least ignore much of what the schools have been saying about the virtues and efficacy of group work in the classroom. The use of groups in the classroom requires a skill that is not easily learned and yet it presents one of the most effective ways in which the teacher can take advantage of the interests of the children in developing the kind of program that will do justice to the child.

Parents and teachers will find the following questions useful in assessing the reading program of the school:

1. Are the basic reading skills taught through all the grades?
2. How many teachers are specifically trained for this job?
3. Are all of the teachers, regardless of their subject, actively involved in teaching the higher reading skills?
4. In the broadest sense, just how well educated is the teaching staff and the school administration?
5. Does the school and the school system have an adequately staffed child guidance program?
6. How many remedial reading teachers are employed in the school?
7. Does the school have a library? How good is it?
8. Are there any provisions for classroom libraries?
9. In the English classes are there any guided free reading programs or is most of the reading confined to single textbooks or a few "graded" sets?
10. Is there any system of referral for children whose reading problems require the services of a psychologist?
11. How effective is the diagnostic testing in the school?

12. How much oral reading does the teacher demand? This is a crucial point. There should be as little as possible. It is a special skill that bears very little relation to useful reading. Where it is not employed as an entertainment device, it is usually mere busy-work.

13. How widely does the English teacher use book lists and how available are the books that are listed?

14. Does she require book reports? They too are almost useless where they are not deadly.

15. Does the teacher respect and accept what the child does read?

These questions are not definitive. Any group of interested people can readily add to them. They can serve to assay the value of a program or to demonstrate the absence of one.

The educational goals that we hold for our children must be far more than mere academic proficiency. Reading, as Bacon said long ago "maketh the full man," but never reading alone. The modern American school is generally fully aware of this fact. The wide ranging curriculum attests to this awareness. Yet, as we have seen at the beginning of this chapter, almost 40 per cent of our children will not graduate from high school. How competent have they become by the time they leave school in the essential skills of the good citizen? Are they capable of finding and using information? Can they make intelligent decisions and act upon them? In short, how well can they "read" the world in which they live?

For the 60 per cent who do graduate and for the less than 30 per cent who do in fact go on to college, have we and the school provided them with the level of reading skill that will make continued education possible? Here we have to distinguish between those relatively large numbers who have learned how to read enough to pass tests and the relatively few who are really capable of learning on their own. The larger group provides all of our professionals. In the main the leaders come from the smaller group. The measure of the excellence of our educational plant is in our ability to increase the numbers of the smaller group. For they are the ones who become truly educated, not in the narrow academic sense of the grad-grind, not as myopic scholars, lost in a welter of filing cards and footnotes. If we are to meet the challenges that face us as a nation today, we have to have people capable of creating compelling ideas. We have to have people whose commitment to our way of life is not based upon blind acceptance but on a broad and brilliant awareness of the working values of our society.

Democracy *is* the better way of life, not because it can produce more refrigerators, but because only through democratic living can we celebrate the wonderful uniqueness of the human being. Democratic living together is not a herd-life. It is a society of equals where special skills and talents may be held and practiced by individuals, but where all ultimately benefit from the efforts of any one. Democracy is not perfect but it is perfectable. In a democracy a mistake is not the ultimate catastrophe although it can be damned uncomfortable. Democracy is makeshift, make-do, trial-and-error, bull-headed hope and careful planning, too. In a democracy anyone may lead for a while, and we are sometimes astounded at our own choices of leadership. But no man or group can ever hold control for private reasons for very long.

If democratic living is valuable to us as individuals and as members of groups, then we have to make certain that every generation will grow beyond our grasp and understanding. Techniques are not enough and the expansion of scientific knowledge is never sufficient. We need to develop the kind of living understanding of the relations of our daily experiences to the total experience of the human race. We need to be able to read widely and wisely in the library of "all our yesterdays" to keep the record of our achievement straight. We need to be able to read accurately the words and features, the hopes and plans of ourselves and our fellow men. We need to be able to live comfortably with beauty, when it is possible, and to deal with the discomforts she puts upon us when there are strange new ways of seeing old things. We must learn how to carve out of each day a place in time where we can wait a while for thought, where we can be quiet with ourselves amid the whirlings and clangings of our ever-new world. We have to master this condition we call leisure and use it as a drawing board for both quick and long-range plans. All this comes hard for us, but we can help our children do it better.

Epilogue

This Is Reading

The act of reading is the act of taking thought about something. The thought may be simply that you wish to be amused or frightened into comfort. It can be the thought that there is some truth to be found that waits in the printed pages. The reading of the printed page can never be the act of a "passive consumer." In fact it is as much a part of the creative act as the author's writing. Where there is a reading man there can be a thinking man, and wherever he exists that part of the world can be better than it is.

Throughout his history man has "read" many things; the flight of birds, the guts of sheep, sunspots, liver spots and the life lines on a hand. He has read the lore of the jungle, the spoor of the beast and the portents in a dish of tea. Whatever he reads and however he has read, his reading has always been done for reasons. When he invented symbols for the words in his mouth and the ideas in his teeming brain, other kinds of reading became useful, desirable and possible. At the beginning this kind of writing and reading was mainly magical. It was converted to practical use when man realized that many of the meanings of many of his words stayed the same for a very long time. They were a kind of memory that never dulled. They could be depended upon to report to tomorrow's children what had happened a long time ago.

We are the inheritors of these reports, and we have enlarged our inheritance. The music of poetry, the pageant of story and drama, the panoply of history, the sunbursts of ideas and the clash of ideals all are woven into the tapestry of our literatures. We have been able to make some of our reading a luxury item for recreation, relaxation and escape. Today this luxury has become a necessity. We need this to keep a buffer between ourselves and the world that sometimes presses in upon us too urgently. Yet all of the reading that we do is, as it has been from the beginnings, rich with purpose. Purpose is, as it must always be, the product of choices between competing alternatives. Purpose is plan, planning and goal seeking. Purpose is a "reason" for acting, and, although this "reason" may begin with mere feeling, it must be thought through in some way if there is to be any hope of reaching our goals.

A distinction has to be made between the different kinds and levels of reading. For mere survival, functional literacy is needed by everyone in our society. High reading efficiency is required of every specialist in his or her own field. Written orders and instructions have to be understood clearly if they are to be carried out. Some people will rarely use reading for anything beyond the simplest source of information. Some may never use it for entertainment. Those of us who find in reading all that has been claimed for it in this book may be unhappy that their interests and preferences are not universally shared. We want the schools to make more people in our image. We will never be satisfied with the schools' success. But we can never afford to believe that the difference between us and all those who do not share our interests is a difference of quality. It is required of us that we respect the differences. The home whose view of the world is only through the tiny picture window of television may not be as rich as ours with its magic casements and grand vistas, but it is peopled by men and women who feel and see and understand that same world. Some of their children can be recruited from their ranks even as we lose some of ours to them. The exchange can be in our favor. It must be if the world is to be better than it is. It cannot be if we protect ourselves from them with ancient outworn intellectual snobberies.

When we deliberately set about teaching a person to read we forget about the goals and concentrate upon the business at hand, the acquisition of skills. This necessity becomes an inescapable fault if it is multiplied in the school when we deal with the young child.

Thinking, of any consequence, is held in abeyance for a while and before we know it, a subtle shift takes place and the children and the teacher too, are interested in reading in order to "get by," to pass up to the next grade, to graduate. Education, despite all our protestations, becomes an assembly-line affair in which the great skills of reading supply the motive power. Almost all of the complaints against the reading performance of children boil down to dissatisfaction over his progress. He is graded, leveled, matched and correlated. The question is not "What is he becoming?" but rather, "How far has he gone?" Comprehension is equated with the ability to regurgitate in their proper sequence, ideas that are not *comprehended* at all. Speed of reading, like speed on the highway, is used as a measure of efficiency and the proper use of power. This is not an objection to reading tests as such, many of them are excellent. It is the use to which they are often put that confounds their authors' plans. Essentially these tests are designed to be used diagnostically. Some teachers use them as a basis for passing or failing the child. In many schools there are few teachers who are even qualified to administer the tests and fewer still who are capable of evaluating them. Reading is more than passing tests and surviving the textbooks, but too many classrooms seem to belie any other aim.

The fault is in the teaching, both at home and in the school. The image of the "scholar" casts its grey shadow across the school years. Some of the children escape by refusal to join the academic ranks, others through their own basic inadequacies. Many knuckle under and accept the narrow requirements and become "good students," some pay their attention fees and no more, reserving to themselves the right to really learn to read. The fault lies in a confusion over what is worth doing, and why. The older educational ideal of the cloistered scholar is not appropriate to the contemporary world. This can be viewed as a misfortune. It is an ideal which cannot be reinstated. Yet many parents and teachers act as if they were preparing the child for just such a life. They often fool themselves by saying that this is precisely what they are not doing. The central aim of our education is not the training of an intellectual elite. That is a special problem, as it always has been, for a special kind of education. Neither is the aim a widespread literary sophistication, although that is not undesirable. We seek to lift the problems that confront them so that their useful lives may be happy.

Once the skills that are basic to reading are acquired (and they ought not to be gained at the expense of purposeful thinking), the rest of our reading life must be an adventure among ideas, feelings and facts. It must relate the life of thought to the life of action. We need not all make our homes in the world of books, but there is no reason for it to be an alien ground. If we are to have free access to this world we must have teachers who are themselves readers, who do not possess trivial minds. Popular education cannot be mass education. We are committed to developing personalities, not products. We need individuals in all their human uniqueness, not two-legged domesticated animals to be fed and raised for a purposeless existence.

There are golden ages yet to be made and times of trouble to be survived. The book is a shield, a tool and a power-pack. It is an instrument for intellectual and emotional navigation. It is man's own sovereign remedy against the ills and confusions of a changing universe. The more competent readers a society has, the greater will be its capacity for doing good to itself. Wakeful happiness should be the best condition of man.